Blockchain Basics

Alexander Tsikhilov

Clink Street

London | New York

Published by Clink Street Publishing 2020

Copyright © 2020

First edition.

ISBN:
978-1-913340-90-2 - paperback
978-1-913340-91-9 - ebook

Table of Contents

Part I
How blockchain is set up

Preface _____ 3
Inventions which changed the world _____ 7
Introduction to the structure of blockchain _____ 13
Decentralization of administration _____ 15
Hashing of information _____ 21
History of cryptography _____ 27
Asymmetric cryptography _____ 31
Digital electronic signature _____ 37
Quantum computations _____ 43
Game theory and blockchain _____ 49
Blocks and their structure _____ 55
Transactions and balances _____ 61

Part II
Practical implementations

Background of the Bitcoin project _____ 69
Mastermind behind Bitcoin _____ 75
How Bitcoin is set up _____ 79
Mining in the Bitcoin network _____ 85
Bitcoin as a cryptocurrency _____ 93
Bitcoin as an asset _____ 99
Bitcoin as an investment _____ 105
Bitcoin as a means of payment _____ 111
Introduction to Ethereum _____ 117
Smart contracts _____ 123
Tokenization _____ 129

Proof-of-stake _____ 135

Altcoins _____ 141

Forks _____ 147

Anonymity in the blockchain _____ 153

Part III
Blockchain industry

Applications of blockchain _____ 161

Blockchain and the state _____ 167

Blockchain and society _____ 173

Investment in ICOs _____ 179

Cryptocurrency exchanges _____ 185

Analysis of the cryptocurrency market _____ 191

Custody of cryptoassets _____ 197

Current issues of the blockchain _____ 203

New world view (conclusion) _____ 209

Part I

How blockchain is set up

Preface

*"First they ignore you. Then they ridicule you. And then
they attack you and want to burn you. And then they
build monuments to you."*

This quotation comes from a speech by the American labor union attorney
Nicholas Klein and is often wrongly attributed – in somewhat different
form – to Mahatma Gandhi. When Klein gave this speech 100 years ago,
the occasion was entirely different; yet, these words also capture of the spirit
of a more recent phenomenon. Not so long ago, a mysterious force charged
onto the scene, bringing in its stead a host of polarized views – ranging from
the categorical rejection of its critics to the emphatic praise of its proponents.
Any phenomenon capable of giving rise to such intense debate is inherently
novel and merits careful consideration. In this case, we're referring to the
technology of blockchain and the technologies based thereon.

Blockchain and its practical implementations in the form of cryptocurrencies
have become the object of heated debate both in the realm of IT technologies
and in the finance industry. The benefits and drawbacks of this technology are
somewhat shrouded by the relatively high level of technical complexity. Those,
however, who manage to apprehend the fundamentals of blockchain networks
often feel that the implications of the advent – and further development – of
blockchain could potentially rewrite the contemporary world order. At such a
thought, some experience elation – and others, despondence. Whereas some
view blockchain as a chance to grow into a new sector, others perceive it to be
a threat to the very existence of the sectors where they currently hold a niche.

In 2008, a certain Satoshi Nakamoto published a document that was
shortly followed by the first practical implementation of blockchain – bitcoin
– and at a global level this went completely unnoticed. The select few who
might have noticed this were just a handful of professional cryptographers
who only paid attention to technical details relevant to their trade. Later,
when the information started being passed around, the project became the

object of mass ridicule – the very notion of a digital currency backed by the electricity consumed during its emission struck many as far-fetched. Yet, these same skeptics changed their tune when the value of a single bitcoin reached multiple thousands of dollars.

In the first half of 2016, blockchain projects started to attract truly massive amounts of attention. At this point, as if bearing out Klein's claim, the industry transitioned into the next phase of its evolution: people began to show resistance. Blockchain-based projects started to pose considerable threats and conflicts of interests for national governments, financial regulators, traditional financial institutions, and large intermediary services. To be fair, many of these threats were entirely legitimate, and several chapters of this book are dedicated to providing an overview and analysis of the issues.

As concerns the critique or generally negative view of the technology, it is admittedly difficult to expect a positive response or support for a phenomenon whose technical workings are so confoundingly difficult to understand. This book aims to explain the technologically complex concepts in as straightforward of language as possible. Moreover, the idea is to present the content in a manner such that readers without a background in computers or finance can develop a working understanding of blockchain fundamentals and the projects based thereon. That said, this work will refrain from using convoluted mathematical devices with sophisticated formulas or overly in-depth descriptions of the algorithms. To a large extent, the more complicated concepts have been paraphrased in a way to present them in "broad brush strokes." It is worth mentioning that the author of this work is neither a mathematician, nor a physicist, nor an economist – moreover, decades have passed since he last worked as a computer programmer. Instead, he is much more an entrepreneur, a cryptoenthusiast, and to some degree a blockchain evangelist.

These prefacing remarks should be borne in mind when considering the information and philosophical positions in relation to the mammoth and captivating phenomenon of blockchain.

A few words on the book's structure. After a brief foray into the history of inventions which at one time or another revolutionized the world, there will be a section dedicated to a detailed description of the blockchain technology. Then, attention will turn to the most popular projects implemented on the basis of blockchain – first and foremost, these are cryptocurrencies. The following part will cover potential applications of the technology in various sectors and will include both descriptions of existing projects as well as some which are still being planned. We have already mentioned the section dedicated to the issues which have arisen in the interaction between blockchain projects and national governments. Of particular interest to many readers will be the following section on investments and cryptoassets. Although many dream of the profits to be had from cryptoinvestments, not all investors are sufficiently aware of what risks this entails or how best to manage such risks. The concluding portion of the book will provide an outlook for the further development of the blockchain technology.

Lastly, it seems appropriate to add a few words on this book's relevance. The blockchain industry and the happenings within it are evolving at a frenetic rate. As such, it cannot be ruled out that at the time of reading this work, certain facts presented herein could be outdated and other half-told stories already complete. That said, this book largely concentrates on fundamental aspects which are unlikely to change significantly with the passing of time. Moreover, the author will largely rely on such descriptions in his presentation of the concepts which comprise the blockchain technology. For the reasons stated above, the hope is that even after the book's release, its contents will remain interesting for readers seeking to learn about such an enthralling topic as blockchain.

The author would like to express his sincere gratitude to his friends and colleagues. Without their help and support, this book would not have been possible.

Inventions which changed the world

The history of human civilization goes back for thousands of years. Over that time, humanity has progressed from the rudimentary techniques and practices of antiquity to the immensely complex technologies of the modern day. The evolution of human civilization has fundamentally rested on a series of pivotal inventions, which each in turn exerted an unspeakable influence on human life and enabled a transition to a more advanced stage of development. The common wheel which appeared more than 6000 years ago drastically simplified the task of conveying people and objects from one place to another. This invention was made possible due to their intuitive understanding of the fact that the frictional force in rotation on a relatively level surface is far less than the frictional force of sliding. Thus, they discovered that it's much easier to use a wheeled cart to transport a load than to drag it across the earth. Around that same time, people began trying to express verbal information in the form of pictures and symbols with the aim of being able to preserve it. In this way, the first buds of written language appeared and therewith the ability to accumulate and share the initial aspects of human knowledge. Some time later, with the establishment of various early forms of governmental structures, humans needed to learn how to account and distribute regulated resources, which gave rise to numbers and elementary arithmetic operations.

The first few centuries of the common era were marked by the military, political, and cultural domination of the Roman Empire throughout Europe, North Africa, and the Middle East. Consequently, it was the Roman numeral system which found widespread use throughout these regions and which continued to be used even following the fall of the empire at the end of the 5th century. However, the non-positional system of numeric notation also had considerable drawbacks, most notably in performing more complicated mathematical operations such as multiplication and division. The development of the exact sciences, the increasing complexity of mathematical devices, and more elaborate means of accounting for resources and their movement laid the framework for social demand for a more advanced counting system: positional notation. On the cusp of the 11th century, the French scholar (and future Roman Pope) Gerbert of Aurillac became one of the first proponents of such a system which he first began using during his studies in Spain, which at that time was largely under Arab rule. Europe was slow to adopt the new system;

indeed, it was not until the mid-13th century, thanks to the efforts of the Italian scholar Fibonacci, that the "Arabic numerals" became relatively commonplace. This largely stimulated the development and advancement of the financial service industry in Europe; this was particularly true of Italy, which became a beacon of financial and technological development in the late Middle Ages.

It was precisely in Italy that the difficulties of accounting for the circulation of physical and financial goods were significantly overcome with the development of double-entry bookkeeping. The method of double-entry bookkeeping rests on the notion of balancing the assets and liabilities. In other words, when altering these values, they must at all times jointly amount to zero. The first instances of ledgers began to appear which contained accounting records (pre-images of transactions) based on the principles of double-entry, in addition to the advent of balance sheets and profit and loss statements. In this manner, the world saw the advent of more advanced means of conducting business as well as the first credit institutions. The first banks are considered to have been set up in medieval Italy – more particularly, the Bank of Saint George in 1407 in Genoa. Thanks to the principle of maintaining double-entry records, income and expenses could be tracked, thus enabling the development of a banking credit system. Banks made active practice of lending money to merchants, nobility, and even European sovereigns. In exchange, bankers secured for themselves not only a considerable income from the interest on the loans, but also substantial political influence, such as the Medici family in Florence whose members ultimately became the dukes of Tuscany and the successive leaders of the entire region.

In 1448, Johannes Gutenberg invented the printing press, therewith again revolutionizing the way that mankind stored and shared its collective knowledge. Strictly speaking, the basics of printing text on paper or fabric had already been in practice for some time – e.g. since the 9th century in China. The only difference was that prior to printing on paper, the text was completely engraved onto a special wooden board, rather than being typed character-by-character. However, when movable type appeared, it provided the flexibility, freedom, and convenience required for book printing to develop more actively. The invention of the printing press made it possible to distribute scientific knowledge with a speed hitherto unknown, which ultimately ushered in the scientific revolution of the modern era. Scientists such as Copernicus, Galileo, and Newton began critically reconsidering the way that their ancestors had understood the order of the world.

From ancient times, humans had endeavored to create mechanisms which did not require human or animal labor. In the second half of the 1st century C.E., the Greek mathematician and engineer Heron of Alexandria (better known for his discovery of the Golden Rule of Mechanics) developed the first model of a steam-powered engine. Despite the engine's extreme simplicity, Heron applied it to develop such devices as a sphere rotated by steam, a mechanism for automatically opening doors, and even a machine for selling "holy water." Given the low level of knowledge sharing at that time, Heron's truly groundbreaking inventions were forgotten for nearly 1700 years, save for a few experiments conducted on steam in the 16th–17th centuries by Egyptian and Italian engineers. It was only in 1781 that the Scottish engineer James Watt patented the steam engine, which essentially paved the way for the English industrial revolution. If Heron's model of the steam engine had received greater attention and not been forgotten for so long, the technological revolution could have taken place much sooner. In such a scenario, one can only wonder whether our history books would speak of the 9th-century rule of Charlemagne as when mankind made its first attempts at space travel. Alas, this is not the only noteworthy invention to have been neglected for such a long period of human history.

In 1936, the Austrian archaeologist Wilhelm König uncovered in the outskirts of Baghdad a curious object – a small ceramic vessel about 13 cm high with a resin-filled neck, from which the tip of an iron rod protruded. Based on the style of ceramics, the find was dated and found to be from the era of the Sasanian Empire (224–651 C.E.). The archaeologist hypothesized that the given vessel was nothing other than a primitive type of galvanized element – i.e. a battery intended for handling electric current. It is not known for certain whether the "Baghdad battery" was indeed used for the supposed purpose. A host of skeptics hold this for entirely unlikely, if only for the fact that no correlating finds exist which the given "battery" could have been used to power. However, some scientists are of the view that the technique of galvanization (using electrolysis to cover one metal with a thin layer of another) was discovered at least 2000 years ago. One way or another, people in Ancient Greece noticed a curious property of electrum: if you rubbed it on wool, it could attract light objects. In this way, humans unintentionally encountered the phenomenon which would later be dubbed "electricity" – i.e. the state from "electrum." As with the steam-powered engine, only in the late 18th century did people undertake systematic studies of electricity, and the fundamental scientific laws relating thereto only appeared a century later. That said, when electricity was harnessed for human use, it drastically altered the face of civilization. Lighting, heating, putting mechanisms into motion, the transmission of information – all this is carried out by means of electricity, and now we cannot imagine their life without this incredibly valuable scientific achievement, which paved the way for even more important inventions.

Studies of electromagnetic radiation by Faraday, Maxwell, and Hertz led to the emergence of devices that make it possible to convey information over a distance – first by telegraph (by wires) and then by radio (wireless).

After this, resistors, capacitors, transformers, electric keys, vacuum tubes, and other electronic components appeared. These were later used as the basis for creating and developing various electrical appliances for both industrial and household appliances. In 1946 in the United States, there appeared the first electronic computational machine ENIAC built with vacuum tubes with a total weight of 27 tons and a computational capacity of 5,000 operations per second. Later, when building computers, the decision was made to stop using the bulky and unreliable vacuum tubes, opting instead for semiconductor technologies. As such, computers started getting smaller in size, while making formidable gains in terms of computational capacity. The invention of the microprocessor in 1971 facilitated the development of personal computers only a few years later. Around this time, initial experiments were conducted on establishing a global telecommunications network for exchanging electronic messages. As these undertakings progressed, they evolved into what we now know as the internet. Thanks to this, mankind acquired the unique ability to quickly amass, distribute, and receive fantastic amounts of information from all domains of human knowledge. Again, the world experienced a technological revolution which radically changed the world at large and thus ushered in another era of human civilization.

By the mid-1990s, the internet had become generally commonplace, and by the dawn of the 21st century, it had become an essential aspect of life for its users. The vast majority of corporate and state bodies established their own online presence – ranging from standard "home pages" to massive portals where one could receive information, order services, and purchase any product imaginable. When social networks came along, the internet made even greater inroads into peoples' daily lives. This actively called into question the viability of traditional forms of mass media – the printed press, television, and radio. It wasn't long before traditional retail began to experience significant competition from online stores. Similarly, the majority of financial operations were now taking place outside of physical bank branches; instead, many people were opting for online banking applications. No longer were phone calls made to financial brokers. Now, these same operations were conducted via online platforms. Now, technology offered users a consolidated and graphic presentation of all the information necessary for making investment decisions, as there was access to pricing, graphs of financial instruments, analytical reports, and market outlooks.

It would be logical to suppose that each of these life-changing inventions did not arise ex nihilo; indeed, they were each proceeded by large-scale, groundbreaking discoveries which form a single uninterrupted chain stretching back through time and connecting the modern world with the beginnings of antiquity. Each of these developments was a response to the needs of civilization which arose under the influence of historical circumstances. This book claims, inter alia, that the historical significance of blockchain stands on par with that of each of the inventions outlined above. The fact that cryptocurrencies were developed on the basis of a distributed register is also a response from civilization to a host of factors which came together in the modern world of finance. The arguments presented in the following chapters aim to demonstrate to the reader the validity of these claims

Introduction to the structure of blockchain

The blockchain technology itself does not contain any fundamentally new or scientifically novel aspects. The operating model of the blockchain derives its value from a combination of various tools, technologies, and principles which – when put together in a certain way – comprise a logical and secure structure for the distributed storage of data. What is blockchain actually? In reality, the blockchain can be compared to a large accounting ledger for recording financial operations conducted between counterparties. However, the ledger is set up in such a way that no entry made can in any way be modified or deleted, as this is inhibited by high-end cryptographic algorithms which are embedded into the technology. The data itself is not stored in a concrete management center, but instead is copied and synced – i.e. replicated between the system participants and network nodes. In this way, any potential changes made to the data by a single user will not be of any notice to the other system participants because the changes violated system protocols.

How is such an "accounting ledger" set up? The "pages" of this ledger are called blocks. In the same way as with pages in a book, the blocks follow one after the other in strict numerical order. Whereas it is possible to tear a page out of a book insert it elsewhere or even throw it away, this is simply not possible with blocks. All the blocks are rigorously linked among one another with special cryptographic "locks," which are phenomenally difficult to hack, even from a theoretical point of view. As the technology is essentially a chain of blocks, it was named "blockchain." In order to be considered a reliable point of data storage, any blockchain structure must meet the following criteria.

- Have a decentralized technological base, i.e. the ability to distribute all necessary data among the network nodes and keep it up to date via the processes of replication and synchronization
- Maintain a continuous connection between the data blocks by creating a link within the block to the one preceding it
- Be able to efficiently encode data sets into unique information blocks of a standard size – i.e. have the ability to hash data
- Apply exceptionally hack-resistant cryptographic algorithms necessary for recording data in the blocks

- Implement elements of the mathematical discipline of game theory to ensure that all the system nodes comply with the established rules and achieve general consensus when creating new blocks and recording new information on them.

All of the tasks listed above comprise the five fundamental pillars of blockchain technology. Throughout the course of the text, greater attention will be given to each of them individually. Some readers could be asking themselves: where is money held on the blockchain? How do is get on to the blockchain, where is it stored, how do you receive it, and how are you later able to spend it? Also, importantly, in what way is this money protected from criminal intrusion? Right now, everyone is talking about "cryptocurrency" which is strongly associated with the blockchain technology. Moreover, most peoples' interest in blockchain – purely from a technological point of view – is secondary. However, in order to profit from investments in cryptocurrencies, it is necessary to understand how they function, if only at a basic level.

In reality, cryptocurrencies are just one of the possible "customizations" of the blockchain structure, i.e. one of its possible pragmatic implementations. History played out in such a way that the very first product to be implemented on the basis of blockchain is a cryptocurrency payment system. Although the system is somewhat lacking in terms of functions, this can certainly be pardoned, given the project's novelty. Despite the fact that the concepts "bitcoin" and "blockchain" came into usage simultaneously, their meanings are far from synonymous, in that the former refers to a cryptocurrency and the latter to the actual technology used to implement the given cryptocurrency. For the record, the term "cryptocurrency" appeared a few years before the actual Bitcoin project – in a 2011 article in Forbes entitled "CyptoCurrency." Satoshi Nakamoto, the author of the Bitcoin project, referred to it as e-cash. We will return to the Bitcoin project, however, in a later section dedicated to practical implementations of the blockchain technology.

Decentralization of administration

Administration is required wherever various elements are connected and operate among one another. Indeed, this is true for all systems, ranging from the social organization of different societies to hardware complexes. Otherwise, the function intended in the planning and development phases could not be guaranteed as most systems lack the capacity to organize themselves in an effective manner. In fact, humans have had to deal with this issue throughout the entire course of their civilization.

When considering the various forms of system management, they can be generally broken down into two basic types: centralized and decentralized. Historically, the earliest form of management of society naturally developed in the days of primitive people, when clans and tribal groups had a strict hierarchy of management within themselves. Yet, as concerned management of the entire population, this could only be viewed as radical decentralization. In most cases, each individual group represented its own management unit, and for this reason it is difficult to represent the entire homo sapiens population as a unified (even if decentralized) system. Indeed, there were no administrative ties between the groups, and when there was any form of interaction, the exchanges were intensely destructive. Typically, the intent was either to destroy or – in the best-case scenario – to forcibly assimilate the weaker groups. As social relations developed between the groups, fixed ties also began to form between them, which ultimately gave rise to more complex hierarchical structures with elements of dominance at the head. When the combined number of the groups cooperating under a single hierarchy became relatively large, the system began to take on more aspects of a centralized model. In other words, the people developed the notion of a "government," at the helm of which there was a single leader – whether elected or ancestral. Such forms of government proved to be entirely viable as it has survived through to the modern era, albeit in somewhat modified form.

Thus, it can be stated that the initially necessary forms of decentralized social organization eventually evolved into a centralized approach, which at that time was more progressive. Centralization made it possible to consolidate resources, which in turn enabled the notion of governmental projects, whether conducting wars of conquest or undertaking colossal construction projects – sometimes, even, both at once! The history of ancient governments like Babylon or Egypt are quite illustrative examples of such. However, in the Medieval Period, other forms of management began to crop up. It should be stated though that these changes were not the result of management principles evolving; instead, in certain instances political circumstances did not permit there to be efficient models of centralized administration.

A salient example can be seen in the Catholic Church which assumed the de facto role of an independent supranational institution – albeit not without a centuries-long struggle – in Medieval Europe. Despite the fact that the inner workings of Catholic Church were dictated by extremely hierarchical notions and the internal management was thus quite centralized, the direct elections of church officials were the product of political consensus between heads of the European powers. The Protestantism which came about in the early Modern Era introduced an undiluted brand of decentralization in its organization of confessional structure. In full spite of the traditional, centralized oversight of the pontificate, there now came a Presbyterian method of managing the church communities.

Governmental structures also began taking their cue from this trend, and in 1291, the European map saw the arrival of the Swiss Confederation – a truly decentralized union of several independent cantons which did not have a central administrative political institute. To this day, Switzerland has not only retained its political sovereignty, but can also boast having one of the most socially affluent populations in the world, which are two phenomenal achievements. Nonetheless, history is also rife with examples where decentralized states existing as feudal factions lost a grip on their power and often met their demise.

These examples clearly demonstrate that one cannot simply claim that one form of government is superior to another. Undoubtedly, both management forms have advantages and disadvantages. Now, it is time to begin drawing analogies between types of social organization and technological systems. The similarity of social and technological forms of administration lie in the common principle of applying to an object the entirety of a subject's administrative activities. As a technological example, let's take the management of the world wide web. Once the internet had penetrated all areas of human life, people began actively using it to organize various services, including commercial, governmental, and social services. Interestingly enough, however, the internet itself is a decentralized structure, despite its having a hierarchical nature at its lower levels of use.

The final user connects to the network via a provider, which likely only has one external channel (unless the provider is quite large) to connect to a larger operator. The larger the subject on the network, the more links it has with other large subjects, in terms of both direct connections as well as cellular exchange points. The largest of operators have their own global infrastructure of trunk lines and supply the largest volume of bandwidth throughput for transmittable data. Nonetheless, the internet does not have a common point of failure. That means that disconnecting one member of the system – even if it is rather large – will not stop the operation of the network as a whole, except for the segment that was completely dependent on the large node which fell out of the network. Yet, in such a case, elements of the segment can switch over to backup channels and thus return online.

Precisely the absence of a common point of failure is one of the main advantages of a decentralized system. Returning to the example of Switzerland, the analogy still holds: in the event of foreign military invasion, neither the federal president nor any other state political institution is allowed to give the order to capitulate. Moreover, even in the ostensible event that such an order is given, residents are legally forbidden from carrying it out. Under such a scenario, a foreign aggressor would be obliged to deal individually with each and every Swiss resident. The same principle applies to the internet. In the unlikely event that some country were to issue a political order to shut down the internet, in all likelihood this would only be technically feasible to carry out on its own territory (with the exception of nodes connected to the internet by satellite, provided that the satellite belongs to another state). Users may also be affected in countries where the trunk lines are connected to transit hubs of the country which has chosen to disconnect from the global network. However, the rest of the global network would remain operational.

In reality, bringing down the internet would require shutting down nearly all of its nodes, and the logistical and technical difficulty of carrying out such an endeavor would border on the essentially impossible. As such, we can speak of a theoretical lack of vulnerability of the network built on the basis of a distributed topology without a single management center. Yet, if we look at the level of web-based services, we will see that the vast majority of them are built on "client-server" technology, i.e. on centralized technology.

For a long time already, many of us have grown accustomed to using various web services. Email support portals, cloud data storage systems (e.g. documents or photos), access to "bank-client" system to manage your accounts and make payments, hotel and airline reservations, trading platforms for transactions in the financial markets, and much more – all these services are built on the basis of a centralized infrastructure. Whenever you use such systems, access to the resources and services first requires visiting a special website of the individual service provider, entering your username and password, and connecting to the central server, where the client's data and assets are stored. However, in instances when the central server goes down for whatever reason, we are not able to use the given service, and we have no option but to wait until the server's functionality is restored. Indeed, this is the main issue with centralized systems: they have a point of failure. Service failure can be the result of various factors: technological problems in the form of hardware failure, errors in the software, abuse within the structure of the service provider itself, various external attacks from hackers or computer viruses. State power or regulatory structures may also exert a negative influence in the jurisdiction where the service provider is physically located.

All of these factors which result in service failure bring one to ponder what technological or organizational measures could be implemented to avoid such scenarios. This question found its response in the appearance of the blockchain technology founded on a decentralized system for saving and exchanging data which precludes all of the negative factors that naturally arise in centralized services. The network topology of a "star"' with rays necessarily coming from all the user nodes to a central point – the server – was replaced by an organizational form, where there is no "central server" per se. Instead, the client nodes interact directly among one another. Such networks are called "peer-to-peer" or "p2p." In such a network, all the nodes typically have equal rights, and any one of them can execute both client and server functions. By thus decentralizing the network topology, the "point of failure" is removed, while also increasing the system reliability and performance to nearly-absolute values.

At this point, readers may find themselves asking a perfectly reasonable question: if the network does not have a server as such, how does such a system save common data, how is this data distributed throughout the network, and in what way is the data protected from unauthorized access or modification? Similarly, how are such systems maintained and developed if all of the participants have equal rights? The blockchain technology provides a solution to most of these issues. The data are replicated between all the system nodes. Protection from modification or unauthorized access to data is provided by mathematical algorithms of asymmetric cryptography. The entire system operates on the basis of an assigned set of rules which all the system participants accept. In the event that significant changes need to be made, the decision is made by a general vote among all the participants.

It's worth mentioning, however, that the administration of decentralized systems is substantially more complicated than is the case with centralized systems. The added complications can be seen as the price to pay for the advantages proffered by decentralization. There still remain many problems which can crop up in the management of decentralized systems. In fact, we will repeatedly return to discussion of this issue in the later chapters.

Hashing of information

The tool of hashing data is an integral aspect of the blockchain technology. Hashing is used to generate addresses in blockchain systems, to form a digital electronic signature of messages, and to produce cryptocoins (i.e. "mining") in some blockchain projects based on the principle of "proof of work." Before considering the above-mentioned elements of blockchain systems, we need to understand what the hashing of data is and upon which principles this procedure is based.

For starters, let's define the term. Hashing is a method of converting a dataset of arbitrary size into a standardized fixed-length string using a special algorithm. That is, if you take a set of data (e.g. the entire text of this book), you can create a digital print of its length, which is perhaps ten characters. In so doing, we must determine a precise algorithm for converting the input data and use it without making modifications for any other data of arbitrary size, whereby we receive a standard string of ten characters. Another way of referring to this is to call it a "deterministic algorithm" because it always yields a predetermined result. The actual result must be a unique representation of the converted input data. For such, we must create a conversion algorithm which will not under any circumstances yield an identical conversion result for different input data sets (i.e. it cannot create "collisions"). Similarly, the slightest change to the input data – even of one bit – must alter the output hash to a state beyond recognition. Here is an example of one of the simplest hashing algorithms (SHA-1), where the pre-images of hashes are two ways of writing the word "decentralization," with only one letter changed in the second word:

As you can see, the second hash has nothing in common with the first despite the minimal difference in the input pre-images. Readers may well ask: why is that even necessary? In reality, hashing is an incredibly useful function which is widely used in computer technologies.

Let's imagine a scenario where we need to transmit a considerable amount of data via communication channels, which for one reason or another may cause interference or distortion. How can we verify whether the final recipient received the data in the original form? Unless we undertake a bit-by-bit comparison of the original information with the information received, we cannot claim with any certainty that the data transfer was error-free. Also, what if someone tampered with the data along the way and deliberately distorted it? Moreover, what is the data set is large enough to be measured in gigabytes? Comparing two blocks of information which are so enormous would take an incredible amount of time. Wouldn't it be simpler to attach to the block of data to be transferred a short unique "digital print" created on the basis of a well-known hashing algorithm? In that case, upon receiving the data, we could simply boot up the same algorithm, feed the same input data into it, and simply compare the resulting hash with the one attached to the transferred data. If they match entirely, this means that the data was transferred without fault and that the data which we have is exactly the same as that sent. This is how we check the integrity of the data. A popular way to use such a certifying algorithm is to obtain the value of the so-called "checksum," which is calculated on the basis of the hashing algorithm of the input data block.

Logically, it would seem that it is absolutely impossible to convert a large block of data into something exceptionally small without losing some of the original information. Indeed, that is so. The hashing algorithm is a one-way mathematical function, the result of which is essentially impossible to convert to the original data prior to conversion. In other words, it is computationally exceptionally difficult to obtain the pre-image of a hash. Theoretically, this is only feasible by sequentially searching through all of the options – i.e. by the "brute force" method. This method is based on the principle of "encrypt and compare:" some assumed input data are hashed and compared with the available hash. If these two hashes do not correspond, this means that the given pre-image does not match. We swap it out and hash it over and over again – ad infinitum – until the hashes suddenly match. Only then can we say that we have "deciphered the hash," but the number of iterations that it would take to achieve this result without exaggeration simply astronomical.

For what it's worth, this method is often used to protect secret passwords under storage on various servers. Openly storing user passwords on internet servers would entail a legitimate amount of risk as criminals could snatch them and then use them to cause material damage to the system and its users. That said, if the passwords are not stored openly as such, but rather as hashes, then the task of achieving unauthorized access becomes considerably more difficult. If the owner enters their password, the system hashes it and compares it with the stored hash for the given user. It they match, this means that the password has been correctly entered and the system authorizes access for the user. If the hashes do not match, the password is incorrect. Even if the criminal has stolen the hashed copy of the password, they are no closer to reaching their aim as their only means of restoring the original password is to perform a large-scale search by trial and error. Therefore, to obtain the original password, it is necessary to use exceptional computing power, which ultimately has a bearing on the total cost of the attack and can render the attack more expensive than the possible material benefit from decrypting the actual password.

Another popular use of the hashing algorithms is in so-called torrent trackers. Torrents are a technology for sharing files – typically media files (in most cases, video files). The technology itself has a hybrid model, whereby torrent files containing technical information are distributed centrally via special torrent tracking portals. Even so, the direct exchange of the primary files takes place centrally via the organization of a direct connection between the "seeders" and the "leechers" – i.e. those who send and receive the files, respectively. Given the volume of data transferred via the internet (other video files can have volumes measured in the gigabytes), these files are transferred in fragments. The task of the receiving party is to contact different senders of fragments of the same file and receive the file in full on their device.

The final goal is to arrange all of these pieces of the original file in such a way that the integrity of the data remains unaffected and that the media player does not identify an error when trying to run the file for viewing. One of the technology's primary functions is to constantly compare large blocks of data with the aim of monitoring their integrity as well as to properly identify their fragments. This is where the hashing function comes into use. The hashes of both entire files and their fragments are used to identify the correspondence of blocks of data to those which were requested. If all the hashes match, this means that we are guaranteed to piece together the file that we need without error. This is how the hashing technology allows users to quickly and reliably compare different blocks of data and guarantee their integrity during transfer.

Finally, hashing is actively being used to streamline the process of searching for data. For this purpose, "hash tables" are generated which contain hashes of various information blocks. They are sorted in a certain order so that when performing a search, you can use the hashes to quickly find data by immediately looking in the right section instead of a large-scale search throughout the entire database.

Now, it is time to consider what mathematical and logical operations are used to calculate the hashes. There are quite a few hashing algorithms, and they range from relatively simple to rather elaborate. Typically, when creating the mathematical model of an algorithm, the goals are to complicate the task of reconstructing in reverse the hash pre-image and to expand the maximum possible range of hashes obtained from the pre-image. This is necessary to ensure that the probability of collisions (i.e. obtaining the same hashes from two different pre-images) is extremely low. Understandably, as the number of bits (size) of the hash increases, the probability of collision exponentially decreases. Nonetheless, in many cases it is necessary to solve a hash task for relatively small sizes as this has an influence on the combined volume of stored information and, consequently, on the cost of storage.

As an example of hashing algorithms, we will present several of the most popular, including those used in various projects based on blockchain technology – e.g. Bitcoin (SHA-256) or Ethereum (SHA-3). The given algorithms are comprised of a certain number of steps (iterations), during each of each various logical operations are performed on the data from the following set.

- **Concatenation**: the "coupling" or "piecing together" two blocks of data when the second becomes a continuation of the first one. One example of concatenation would be "1111'" and "2222" which yields "11112222."
- **Addition**: a basic mathematic operation for two or more numbers.
- **Conjunction** (or **Logical AND**): the result of this bitwise operation will be true (1) if and only if both bits are 1. Otherwise, the result is false (0).
- **Disjunction** (or **Logical OR**): the result of this operation will be true (1) if at least one of the arguments is true (1). Otherwise, the result is false (0).
- **Exclusive logical XOR**: the result of this operation for two bits will be true (1) if and only if one of the arguments is true (1) and the other false (0). Otherwise, the result is false (0).
- **Logical negation NOT**: a bitwise inversion resulting from a unary operation, where the resulting bit will always have the opposite value of the input bit (i.e. ones become zeros and vice versa).

- **Bitwise shifts**: when the bit values are moved into the neighboring registers in accordance with the direction of the shift (e.g. for the block "10100110," the result of a logical shift to the left would be "01001100."

Bitwise shifts can be logical (when the last bit in the direction of the shift is lost and the first becomes a zero) and circular (when the last bit in the direction of the shift assumes the place of the first). The example given above illustrates a logical shift as the result of a circular shift to the left would have yielded the result "01001101." In addition, a set of auxiliary constants assigned to each algorithm can be used within each iteration. These constants are used in the various operations described above. In this way, each step of the algorithm takes the result yet further from the input data. This complex cyclical mixing of data is called hashing, a word perhaps intended to convey a notion of "mishmash." With hashing – much like in English cuisine – the individual ingredients (pre-image) of a "mash" can hardly be determined from the finished product. However, from the very beginning, there have been attempts to find efficient methods for recovering pre-images for the various hashing algorithms.

In order to get a feel for the problems associated with the cryptographic stability of the most popular hashing algorithms, let's take a look at the calculations of the variety of hashes and the probability of finding collisions for them. The correlation between the number of bits (size) of the hash n and the number of possible outputs (variations of hash generation) is equal to $2n$. With an average hash length in the most prominent blockchain projects being 256 bits, these means a number outputs equal to 2^{256} or approximately 1.2×10^{77} which is on par with the estimated number of atoms in the visible universe. Yet, it is not necessary to comb through all of the different variants in order to find a collision.

There is a well-known attack algorithm called the "birthday attack" which is based on a paradox associated with determining the probability of two individuals in a group of N people having the same birthday. The paradox lies not in determining the probability of a particular person in the group having the same birthday as someone else in the group (the probability of such would be quite low in small groups), but rather the probability of any two people in the given group having the same birthday. This probability is already of a completely different order. For example, in a group of 23 people, the probability of such would be greater than 50%, and in groups of 60 people or more the probability already exceeds 99%. The situation is similar with collisions in hashing algorithms, albeit with significantly larger numbers. Yet, the general idea remains the same: in order to find a collision with any significant degree of probability, far fewer variants need to be cycled through than the maximum number of theoretically possible outputs. The number required to have a 75% probability of finding a collision for 256-bit key is 5.7×10^{38}, which is smaller by a factor of 10 to the 39th power than the mathematically largest number of possible outputs. As you can see, even with such significant reductions, the computational complexity of sorting through all of the variants remains exceptionally high. Therefore, blockchain technologies use hashing algorithms with a large number of bits to protect the stored data from attempts of fraudsters – at least until computational capacities overcome these barriers of complexity.

We have tried to look at the fundamental aspects of the principles of hashing. We will consider direct applications of this process in later sections of the book which focus on practical implementations of blockchain projects.

History of cryptography

When looking at the nitty-gritty of blockchain, it would be unthinkable to skip over one of its most critical components: cryptography. Cryptography in the blockchain is a connecting element of exceptional force on which rests the basic value of the distributed ledger technology as a whole. Indeed, cryptography is responsible for ensuring the integrity and transfer of data as well as ownership rights and for protecting assets held in the user network – primarily financial assets. Indeed, blockchain owes its very existence to cryptographic technology as without it, blockchain would no longer have any benefits to offer its users and its very use would be pointless. How could cryptography be so important? It's time to break down the subject of cryptography and how it became the vital core of the blockchain technology.

The history of cryptography goes back several millennia. Since times ancient, humans have had the need to transmit secret information over a distance. Most typically, this related to information of military significance. In an era where collective security arrangements were still unheard of, militarily weaker nations were constantly preyed upon by their more aggressive neighbors. In order to preserve their freedom and independence, the only option available to smaller states was to partner with strong allies. However, to conclude such an agreement required exchanging information which could not under any circumstances be divulged a potential enemy. This was also true for orders given by military command to its units located at a great distance from the main forces: to ensure continuous coordination, information had to constantly transmitted concerning location, numbers, and supplies, not to mention the tactics and strategy for upcoming military actions.

There were specially trained individuals – messengers or spies – responsible for quickly conveying the information to the final destination without being noticed by the adversary. Nevertheless, the envoy invariably ran a considerable risk of being intercepted, at which point the information in their own keeping would be in the enemy's keeping. To mitigate such risks, the messages were almost never composed in straightforward text, but rather were encrypted in one way or another. This practice relied on the assumption that the key for encryption was available exclusively to the sender and the intended recipients. As such, before messages could be exchange, some initial effort had to be spent distributing encryption keys between the center and its potential recipients

Accordingly, there was an ever-present risk that the information could be intercepted (or purchased) and subsequently used to decrypt the enemy's messages. Admittedly, the sender would never become aware of this because the enemy would never voice the fact that they possessed the secret key.

When both the sender and the recipient use the same key for encrypting and decrypting the messages exchanged between them, this is called symmetric cryptography because there is explicit symmetry in the encryption keys. This method of encryption was used throughout nearly all of human civilization – starting in antiquity and continuing through the 1970s. What techniques were used for encryption? As with other spheres of human knowledge, cryptographic technologies underwent their own evolution. In the very beginning, people would, quite simply, substitute some of the letters in the message with others. For example, the Roman commander Gaius Julius Caesar encoded messages to his generals by shifting the letters by three positions in the Latin alphabet – i.e. the letter "B" became "E," "C" became "F," etc. Such ciphers that relied on rote substitution were called monoalphabetic. These monoalphabetic ciphers would later be replaced by polyalphabetic ones, whereby several monoalphabetic ciphers were applied in turn to the letters of the text being encrypted. In one form or another, this method continued being used for nearly a millennium, until the early 20th century when electromechanical devices started being used for encrypting messages. Perhaps, the most famous implementation of this cryptographic method was the German rotary cipher machine called Enigma, whose ciphers were considered uncrackable.

From a contemporary perspective, Enigma does not seem nearly so cryptographically robust. However, at the time of the Second World War, this machine managed to generate a fair amount of trouble for the parties opposing Germany. In 1932, long before the outbreak of military hostilities, the Polish intelligence agency managed to obtain from their German agents a few codes and the operating principles of the machine. This information made it possible for them to create a replica machine in their laboratory and begin studying how the algorithm operated. In 1939, Germany invaded Poland; however shortly beforehand all the work on Enigma had been passed off to British intelligence who in turn set up a special group to decipher messages, into which they recruited the exceptionally talented mathematician and cryptographer Alan Turing. By 1940, Turing's team had managed to construct about 200 cryptanalytic machines operating with the Enigma cipher, but for a long time the sheer number of variants requiring an exhaustive search for decryption effectively ruled out the possibility of cracking the code. Nonetheless, Turing did indeed identify certain phrases which repeated throughout the encrypted messages. For example, knowing that the Nazi greeting could be found in essentially all correspondence made it possible to drastically reduce the range of options for inspection and, ultimately, to crack the code. Some hold the view that this very event in no small way brought on Germany's defeat, and some historians make the further claim that it shortened the war by at least one year.

By the second half of the 20th century, scientists were increasingly convinced that symmetric cryptography was insufficient for coping with a number of modern problems. The advent of computers and their heightened computational capacity meant that it no longer posed any serious difficulty to hack even the most complex symmetric ciphers in use at that time. For this reason, the world undertook a gradual transition to mathematical cryptography. This transition gave rise to a legitimate revolution which opened a fundamentally new chapter in the history of cryptography. The product of this revolution was asymmetric cryptography or, in more common parlance, public-key cryptography.

In 1976, two cryptographers by the names of Whitfield Diffie and Martin Hellman published a paper entitled "New Directions in Cryptography." The main idea of the paper was a method whereby in addition to a secret key, there was also a public key which was mathematically connected to the secret one. Furthermore, the process of determining the private key from the public one was a problem of exceptional mathematical complexity. As a result, it became possible to distribute the secret key even via insecure channels without running any risk of revealing it to third parties. Thus, the parties needed only to swap the public keys along with the auxiliary information for calculation purposes. Then, via a set of mathematical operations, the recipient could recover the common secret key. This algorithm would be dubbed the "Diffie–Hellman key exchange" in honor of its creators and would usher in a cryptographic era where the encryption algorithms developed would boast incredibly impressive levels of cryptographic security. As an aside, these same algorithms would later come into use in blockchain technologies.

How does public-key encryption work? In reality, the operating principle is rather straightforward – each user generates their own secret key (even randomly). Then, depending on the specific encryption algorithm, certain mathematical operations are used to generate a public key on the basis of the secret one. This means that the owner can freely distribute the public key – i.e. place it on the internet, in personal correspondence, or even in the newspaper. Indeed, one needs to disclose the public key because whoever may want to send a message to the key's owner will require it in order to encrypt the message. Here's the catch: in order to decipher a message encoded with the public key, only the corresponding private key will do the trick. It should be evident that the convenience of such a system far outweighs that of symmetric cryptography, where the constant need to distribute a shared secret key via insecure channels constitutes a veritable vulnerability for encryption technologies as a whole.

Yet, it should be stated that even today symmetric encryption systems continue to be used. This fact owes to the exceptional speed, with which symmetric algorithms can perform encryption and decryption. In systems where speed is operationally critical and the parties can ensure secure transfer of the private keys among themselves, the choice to use symmetric encryption can be not only efficient, but also fully justified. Quite often, data is transmitted on the internet via a combination of asymmetric and symmetric cryptography algorithms. More specifically, when connection is established, the Diffie–Hellman algorithm is used to exchange the common secret key, and after that, both parties use the common secret key as the key for encrypting and decrypting data packets with symmetric algorithms. That said, in distributed systems with a large number of users – including blockchain projects – asymmetric cryptography is the unquestioned norm. What methods of asymmetric cryptography are currently the most popular?

Asymmetric cryptography

There are quite a few asymmetric cryptography algorithms. However, in this work, we will only consider a handful of them, starting with some simpler examples before moving on to more elaborate ones. The Diffie–Hellman algorithm which was the first asymmetric cryptography technique did not address the issue of authenticating parties who jointly generated a secret key. However, as early as in 1977, an algorithm appeared which could not only encrypt, but could also authenticate system subjects by using a digital electronic signature. This algorithm was built on a problem called "factorization" of large integers and was given the name RSA, an acronym of the founders' last names – Ronald Rivest, Adi Shamir, and Leonard Adleman. Factorization is the process of breaking a natural number down into a product of prime factors. In the RSA algorithm, two large prime numbers are used for the private key, and the public key is the product of those two numbers. Cryptography makes use of this method due to the fact that multiplying several numbers together does not require a large effort, even if they are very large. That said, the inverse operation of factorization the resulting number is a problem which entails a hefty degree of computational complexity.

Let's take a look at an example. Let's say that we have three prime numbers – 3, 5, and 7. By definition, prime numbers are only divisible by themselves and one. If we multiply these three numbers together, we get a result of 105. Now, let's imagine that we can only see the final answer of 105 and that now, working backwards, we need to break this number down into its prime factors – i.e. the original numbers 3, 5, and 7. Humans can have some difficulty in solving this problem even with elementary three-digit numbers. However, factorizing numbers with a string length dozens of numbers long is no trivial matter even for a modern computer. Admittedly, certain algorithms have found a more efficient approach to the task of factorization than merely conducting an exhaustive search through all divisors; however, to date no truly optimal algorithm exists which is capable of quickly performing this task for large numbers.

The issue of factorization has occupied scientists for centuries, and one of the first people to tackle this problem was the French mathematician Pierre de Fermat. As early as 1643, he proposed a factorization method which still today is put to use in RSA cryptanalysis ciphers. It should come as no surprise that for any encryption algorithm, there will always be people looking for ways to successfully attack it. For some people, this is a criminal endeavor, whereas for others it's scientific: they want to ascertain the cryptographic security of the algorithm in order to protect projects built on it. Back in the mid-2000s, reports began arising that a group of scientists from one university or another had cracked first the 512-bit and then the 1024-bit RSA key. Moreover, they managed to do so in an entirely reasonable amount of time without making use of any exceptional computational capacity. Of course, no single computer – even the most powerful one – could cope with such a computational load on its own, so to solve such problems, computers are usually grouped into special computing clusters.

Over the past ten years, the computational capacity of computers has made notable leaps. According to Moore's Law, the performance of computer processors doubles every 18 months, which means that the length of the public key must be constantly lengthened in order to maintain the cryptographic stability of the RSA algorithm in various technological solutions. Since public keys cannot be endlessly lengthened, people began to discard this algorithm in favor of more progressive solutions capable of providing acceptable levels of cryptographic security with keys having a string length of 256-1024 bits. An example of a more progressive solution was the DSA digital signature based on the discrete logarithm model. This algorithm uses modular arithmetic, which is the task of finding the power to which you need to raise a given number in order to obtain a certain remainder after performing modular division by another given number. The following example will better illustrate the point:

$$3^x \bmod 17 \equiv 13$$

Modular division is the standard process of dividing one integer by another with an integer remainder. Children learn a similar version of this mathematical operation at school before they move on to the subject of fractions. After that, however, they happily neglect division with a remainder for many years until they get to advanced mathematics courses in university, where it suddenly turns out that division with a remainder indeed has an important role to place in number theory and algebra. In the given example, we need to determine what power to raise the 3 such that when we divide the result by modulo 17, we get 13 as the remainder. Correct answer: x = 4 That is, $3^4 = 81$, 81/17 = 4 +

remainder 13 (double check: 4 x 17 = 68 + 13 = 81). That wasn't so hard, was it? By raising the 3 to various powers x (from 1 and up) and then diving the result by modulo 17, we will get a different remainder each time. However, the remainders will all have one thing in common: they will all fall in a range from 1 to 16, even if they are not arranged in order (with the sequential increase of the power x). A set of these numbers is called a quotient ring. It is called a ring because the remainders will constantly repeat for various values of the power x to which the base number is raised. Let's now imagine that we are not working with one-digit or two-digit numbers, but rather with very large numbers. In such cases, if we don't know the power of the given number ahead of time, then finding it for specific values of remainders can become exceedingly difficult. This is the very complexity at the heart of the DSA algorithm.

As mentioned above, all such encryption algorithms are built on a task that can be easily and quickly solved in one direction, but that is exceptionally difficult to solve in reverse. This is also true of the DSA algorithm. If we attempt to solve the problem by brute force (i.e. simply iterating through all the different values), this method will require an inordinate amount of time. Therefore, instead of the standard exhaustive search method, algorithms have been developed that approach this problem much more efficiently. Indeed, the success has been such that taking into account the constant increase in the performance of modern computers, mathematicians have been forced to think about the need to ratchet up the complexity of the encryption algorithm. Otherwise, they could find themselves facing a situation where ciphers are being hacked en masse in the relatively near future.

To lend an added degree of complexity to the problem, in 1985 a discrete logarithm algorithm was developed on the basis of elliptic curves – the elliptic curve digital signature (ECDSA) algorithm. What is this about and what type of curve is it? An elliptic curve is a set of points described by the equation $y^2 = x^3 + ax + b$. To put it another way, these operations are performed not on a ring of numbers as in the DSA algorithm, but rather on the set of points of an elliptic curve, which significantly complicates the task of recovering the private key from the public one. Here is an example of a normal elliptic curve:

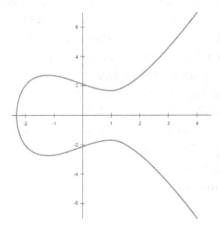

On a set of points belonging to an elliptic curve, points can be selected such that it is possible to add them to themselves and obtain the answer expressed as another point on the same curve. In other words, this means solving the equation X = nP, where n is equal to 2 and greater, and X and P are points on a given curve with coordinates on the x and y axes. Multiplying by the constant n is nothing more than performing an addition operation n number of consecutive times. This way, we start with the fact that we need to add the starting point to itself and get the result in the form of the same point, but with different coordinates. Geometrically speaking, adding a point on an elliptic curve to itself means constructing a tangent to a given point. Then, we find the point where the tangent intersects with the curve graph and build a vertical line from it, which thus enables us to find the point of its intersection on the reverse side of the curve. This point will be the result of addition. Geometrically, such operations look as follows:

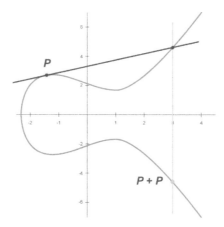

In the following iteration, the starting point will then be the one obtained in the previous step. From this point, we construct a new tangent and repeat n number of times. The complexity of the task lies in the inverse search n for the known points X and P, and this problem does not have a quick solution. In the given example, n would be the secret key and X – the public key. Obviously, the computer does not perform the operation of addition geometrically, but rather algebraically. Special formulas exist for such which are based on the available coordinates for each of the points on the x and y axes.

As a side note, not all forms of elliptic curves would be suitable foundations on which to base cryptographic algorithms. In this sense, there are rather "weak" elliptic curves which do not offer sufficient stability for the various algorithms used to solve the discrete logarithm problem. As such, in order for an elliptic curve to be suitable for complex cryptographic tasks, it must satisfy various requirements, which we will not consider here, so as not to overly complicate the description of general principles.

Algorithmic theory has identified various categories of complexity of solving mathematical problems: polynomial, sub-exponential and exponential. The complexity of discrete logarithm algorithms based on elliptic curves is increasing at an exponential rate. So far, no solution for this problem has been developed even in sub-exponential time – i.e. in a time proportional to a function which increases more slowly than any exponential function. For this reason, this algorithm has now come into quite widespread use as a model with relative cryptographic security which uses keys with a comparatively small number of bits. If we compare these two algorithms with one another, in instances when the length of the public RSA key or the standard DSA is 1024 bits, a string length of only 160 bits will suffice for an algorithm using elliptic curves to achieve comparable cryptographic security. The difference in efficiency is obvious, so most popular blockchain projects – such as Bitcoin or Ethereum (and many others) – use cryptography on elliptic curves, which is currently acknowledged as the most reliable.

In addition to the actual data encryption procedure, the most important element associated with encryption in blockchain technology is the digital electronic signature. What is it and how is it used?

Digital electronic signature

The familiar concept of "signature" is as old as time itself – since antiquity, humanity has faced the issue of verifying the authenticity of documents. Some elements used to complicate the forgery of documents included unique forms of the name of the official, merchant, feudal lord or even the monarch made by the author himself. This was done sometimes in combination with wax seals bearing the imprint of the signatory's state or family coats of arms. It was believed that this combination significantly hindered third parties from creating unauthorized reproductions of the documents for their own purposes. In the majority of cases, these protective measures actually did work. However, there could be no guarantee that some medieval attacker specially equipped for such instances would not be able to put together a relatively accurate copy of the original.

With the advent and development of computer technologies, the question of authenticity of information transferred via telecommunication channels became most acute – after all, it is much easier to forge an unprotected digital document than a handwritten one. For this reason, computer documents were printed out, signed by hand, and in most cases received an ink stamp. Then the document was scanned and sent as a graphic image containing both a printed and human-made insignia. Yet, even this could not perfectly rule out the possibility of counterfeits – at least not until technology made the qualitative leap of creating documents with a digital e-signature generated by asymmetric cryptographic algorithms.

A digital electronic signature is created by a certain cryptographic algorithm with the input of two necessary elements: the hash of the data set to be signed and the private key of the signature's owner. A digital signature offers a number of useful properties; most importantly, only the owner of the private key (and no one else) can generate a signature. To be more precise, computational attempts may be made to determine the secret key on the basis of the public key, but as we have already discussed, this is a task of exceptional difficulty and where the probability of success borders on naught. The authenticity of a digital signature can be verified if one knows the public key of the signature holder. Moreover, a document bearing a particular signature cannot be altered at all – even by a single bit – since the signature would thus lose its validity. Any change to the document would trigger a change in the hash, which is critical for the generation of the signature itself. In short, a digital signature not only identifies the author, but also assures the integrity of the document on which it is placed.

To generate a digital signature, the first thing needing to be done is to choose a cryptographically secure asymmetric algorithm. This will then be used to create a secret key and a public key. After that, the hash needs to be calculated for the block of data to be signed – e.g. a document – once a suitable hash function algorithm has been selected. Hashing serves two purposes: protecting the integrity of the original data and creating a digital fingerprint in a standardized form. At this point, with the data hash and the private key on hand, we run the algorithm for generating the digital signature and receive a data string, as a result. The process of verifying the signature and the integrity of the signed data in different encryption algorithms differs mathematically from one to the other. However, the general principle of verification is to calculate the two results obtained in different ways; moreover, one of them can only be obtained with the public key of the signatory. Then, these results are compared, and in the event of discrepancy, the signature is deemed to have been forged or changes to have been made to the original data after signing.

We will take the RSA algorithm as an example. A comparison is made of the hashes of the signed data set, where the first hash is obtained in the standard way as a result of the hash function on the source data and the second is calculated using the public key. Then, the two resulting hashes are compared, at which point conclusions can be drawn concerning the signature's authenticity – i.e. its mathematical conformity to the signed data. It should be again emphasized that the generation of a digital signature or the procedure of verifying it is carried out using mathematical operations unique to a specific encryption algorithm selected beforehand. Generally speaking, factorization or discrete logarithm algorithms are used for this purpose, including on a set of points on elliptic curves. This latter method is generally standard in blockchain environments as it is considered the most cryptographically secure. The diagram shows a sample use of an RSA algorithm to sign and verify a signature:

Signing

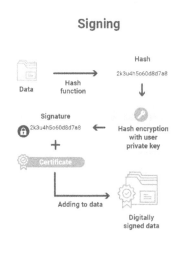

Verification

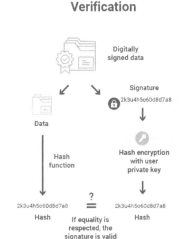

It should also be noted that a digital signature is not necessarily based on asymmetric encryption algorithms. Methods also exist for using symmetric systems to generate digital signatures. In such a case, a third party is required to act as an arbiter with the trust of both parties and who holds the shared secret key. Given the lack of effective algorithms and the need for unconditional trust in the third parties, this method is rarely used. For this reason, asymmetric encryption algorithms are much more commonly used, and in blockchain projects they are exceedingly prevalent.

In addition to the standard form of digital signature, various implementations of blockchain projects employ some more exotic forms. For example, there is the "blind signature" which is also known as a "zero-knowledge proof." The blind signature algorithm is simple: one member of the system encrypts their message and sends it to another member who is a trusted node (trusted by some set of other nodes) in the system. This entrusted participant places their signature on the encrypted message without actually having any knowledge of its contents. The signed message is then returned to the original sender who again decrypts it, leaving only the signature of the entrusted node. This could be likened to a situation where a trusted participant receives a sealed envelope containing both a message sheet and a copy sheet. Without opening the envelope, the recipient places their signature on it, which automatically transfers the signature to the sheet bearing the message via the copy sheet. Once the envelope is returned to the sender, the sender removes the signed message, thereby receiving the desired result – obtaining a signature from a trusted node without disclosing the message itself. Such an operation can be performed mathematically using asymmetric cryptography protocols – e.g. the RSA factorization algorithm.

For what purpose are such elaborate techniques used? In fact, examples abound. For example, there are ballot boxes at elections. To receive a ballot, a voter must have their identity verified by an employee of the election committee who in turn will not be able to see in favor of whom or what the voter places their vote. By using blind signature technology, one has the guarantee that only properly identified and eligible voters receive ballots. The result is confidence in the election results because society trusts in the staff of election committees. The electronic voting system works on a similar principle, whereby the node responsible for verification signs a message from the voter which it identifies (containing encrypted information about their vote) and then returns the signed message to them. In this case, the signature indicates that a trusted node of the network duly verified the voter's right to participate in the vote. Upon receiving a signed copy of the message, the voter sends it to the address of a special counter which registers this vote as legitimate and in favor of one of the candidates. Many countries are already implementing similar algorithms in their elections to various authorities, ranging from municipal structures to national parliaments. Estonia is the most famous country to use internet voting based on national identity cards, with this procedure first used in the 2007 parliamentary elections.

Another interesting way to generate a digital signature is the "ring signature." Even in the 17th century, when lodging complaints with their superiors, British soldiers would sign in a ring around the text of the statement itself. This unusual form of signature was used to make it impossible to determine who signed the document first – the individual whom officers would presume to be the instigator. American soldiers would later adopt this method – in particular at the end of 19th century during the Spanish-American war in Cuba. When electronic systems appeared which made it possible to sign different data blocks, it became situationally necessary to mask a particular signatory in the list of other potential candidates. For this purpose, a special mathematical algorithm was developed that generates a certain set of public keys associated with the various participants in the system.

Typically, most of the network participants involved do not have the slightest idea that their public key could be used to generate a ring signature.

In the set of public keys thus obtained, only one of them is paired with the corresponding secret key since it is operated by the signatory themselves who wishes to remain anonymous to all others. The ring signature itself is generated by feeding into the algorithm a set of public keys (one of its own and many others), its own private key, and the message to be signed. The signatory receives the data string of the ring signature as the output. Any other system participant can verify this signature by using a special algorithm which uses all the same data, except for the secret key as this is known to the signatory alone. Blockchain systems use algorithms for generating a ring signature to provide additional anonymity if the users deem the technological level of privacy to be insufficient. In the section on the problem of anonymity in the blockchain, consideration will be given to such cryptocurrency projects.

Finally, there is a system for consolidating electronic signatures from different participants which is called "multi-signature." In some situations, it can become necessary to manage digital assets on the basis of decisions made simultaneously by multiple system participants. There could, for example, exist an electronic account containing a substantial amount of money which belongs to a group of participants or even a legal entity. The system rules stipulate the total number of account managers as well as the percentage value of the signature weight assigned to each of them. Another option offered is that any transfer from one account to another must be confirmed by at least 60% of the weighted participation of all managers. In a scenario with three managers with equally weighted signatures (33.3% respectively), it is necessary for at least two participants to digitally sign a money transfer (33.3% x 2 = 66.6% > 60%) in order to fulfill the threshold condition. This practice exists in blockchain systems due to the technological impossibility of undoing completed transactions. As such, any decision to transfer a large sum of money held collectively must be made in such a way that no single individual can abuse their management authorizations. Multi-signatures can be implemented in blockchain projects by using various mathematical methods on the basis of asymmetric cryptography algorithms.

The identification and protective function of the electronic signature enable a vast range of use in everyday life – primarily in the legal and business spheres. Currently, digital signatures have found application as a means of remotely identifying counterparties in various agreements – from the establishment of new enterprises to the acquisition of large assets, including real estate. Some governments have made electronic signatures legally equivalent to conventional signatures. The digital signature technology, more at the multi-signature algorithm, is frequently used in "escrow services." When important transactions are being concluded, these services are rendered by a third party responsible for arbitration whose signature attests to the proper performance of obligations by the transaction counterparties. Various algorithms for generating digital signatures are quite common in blockchain environments. As the cornerstone of the entire technological process, digital signatures guarantee ownership rights for cryptoassets to users of the distributed network and protect the integrity of the information placed in the system. Unquestionably, security issues and ensuring the lack of hackable vulnerabilities in this method of protecting information are central concerns.

In the previous chapter, we mentioned that the first proposed public key encryption algorithm (Diffie–Hellman) did not provide the digital signature functionality. However, the factorization or discrete logarithm algorithms which followed – including elliptic cryptography – are optimally suited for this purpose. Nonetheless, one should not be overly certain that even such cryptographic algorithms like the ECDSA have exceptionally bright prospects because scientists are hard at work on a massive surprise for the cryptography industry: quantum computers. These elaborate computational devices could pose legitimate difficulties for all mainstream encryption algorithms. What is a quantum computer and what difficulties does it pose for cryptographic algorithms?

Quantum computations

The possibilities of breaking cryptographic algorithms – more at, to recover a secret key from a private one – have always been limited by the computational capacity of computers. Processor performance has grown steadily over the years, but so has the cryptographic security of algorithms. In other words, the difficulty of hacking is increasing on a daily basis, and there is no end to this race in sight. However, in recent years, the technological companies manufacturing the electronic components on integrated circuits – primarily microprocessors – began to clearly perceive the physical limitations of further reducing the size of the transistor as the basic element of the electronic circuit. As of 2018, the latest developments in semiconductor technology make it possible to massively produce microprocessors on the basis of the 10-nanometer (nm) production method. At least, the company Samsung is already using technology in its smartphones, whereas Intel continues to use 14-nm processors for personal computers. In both cases, the technology for manufacturing transistors is gradually reaching atomic dimensions despite the fact that a transistor can clearly not be made out of a single atom.

The latest scientific news report that scientists have managed to create a transistor of a mere seven atoms; however, it is hardly possible to further reduce this number. The fact is that a single silicon atom is estimated to be 0.2-nm; however, it is also believed that the smallest conceivable gate size of a silicon transistor is 5-nm. What does that mean? This implies that the renowned Moore's Law – which states that the processor performance doubles every 18 months – has essentially reached its physical limits. This will, in turn, have an impact on the maximum computational capacity of computers which will no longer increase proportionally as was previously the case. As a result, endeavors to break cryptographically secure encryption algorithms will gradually cease to make progress, and all ongoing projects built on the basis of such algorithms will finally feel safe. Yet, how can we be certain that this will happen?

If classical technologies for manufacturing computers reach their physical limits of development, then solutions to ensure a long-term increase in performance must be sought out in fundamentally new scientific and technological areas. One of the areas offering the greatest prospects for significant growth in computational performance is currently considered to be quantum computers.

Quantum computers are computational devices which are radically different from the binary logic to which we are accustomed. Classically speaking, the smallest cell of memory – called a bit – can assume stable values of zero or one. Quantum computers have quantum bits, also known as "qbits". Qbits can be, for example, the spin directions of subatomic particles as well as various states of external electrons or photons. In order to avoid delving into the nuts and bolts of quantum mechanics, we will not look very closely at the physical structure of a quantum computer; instead, we will note a few of the properties which set it apart from a classical computer.

In 1931, the Austrian physicist Erwin Schrödinger put forth a thought experiment in which he placed a hypothetical cat into a steel chamber containing a device with a radioactive atomic core as well as a flask with poisonous gas. The experiment conditions prescribed a 50-percent probability of core decay within one hour. In the event of such, a mechanism is triggered which breaks the flask, after which the cat dies. However, if the core does not disintegrate, then the cat remains safe and sound. The point of this experiment is that the outside observer can never know with any certainty whether the core is intact and the cat alive without opening the box. Until such time, the cat is presumed to be simultaneously alive and dead.

Obviously, no entity in our world can be in two states at the same time. Therefore, it would be more correct to say that the cat is in a state of "superposition," in which all possible versions of the state are admitted with varying degrees of probability. That said, the sum of the probabilities of all possible states must equal 100%. This can also be attributed to how the quantum bit of a quantum computer operates – in the exact same manner, it be in a state of superposition, taking both the values of logical zero and one. Until the moment when the state of the quantum bit is directly measured, its exact value remains unknown to the observer, and after obtaining the measurement result, the qbit is immediately fixed in the definite state of one or zero. Admittedly somewhat strange at first glance, this property of qbits proved quite useful in the organization of parallel calculations of complex computational problems, including cryptographic algorithms.

Another interesting feature of qbits is that they can go into a state of quantum entanglement, where a change in the state of one bit automatically entails the opposite change in another connected bit. However, arranging a quantum entanglement of many qbits among themselves is a colossally tall order from a technological point of view as this requires isolating the bits from all forms of interference in the surrounding environment. At the moment, leading manufacturers of quantum computers, such as Google, have managed to keep as many as 72 bits in a connected state, which currently holds the status of a world record. Is 72 bits a big or a small number in terms of breaking, let's say, the RSA factorization algorithm? If we consider n ordinary bits, then only one of the 2^n possible states can be selected at a single moment in time, while n qbits in the superposition state will simultaneously be in 2^n states. As such, linear growth in the number of qbits will be accompanied by exponential growth in the number of possible states. In turn, this signifies that a quantum computer with a large number of qbits would have exceptional computational capacity. Taking into account the most recent developments in the field of quantum computing, experts estimate the capacity of a quantum computer to be billions of times greater than that of a conventional one. The chief advantage of quantum computing, however, will be in solving mathematical problems requiring brute force to pore through large numbers of options.

Perhaps even such substantial computational capacity will still prove insufficient for easily cracking public key encryption algorithms. The number of qbits required for such would be much greater: for example, for the RSA factorization algorithm with a 2048-bit key, the number of qbits necessary would be two times as much. These data are calculated on the basis of computational requirements of a hybrid (containing both classical and quantum parts) algorithm, presented in 1994 by Peter Shor, an American scientist who specialized in the field of quantum informatics. Oddly enough, the number of qbits required to crack elliptic cryptography would be fewer: for 256-bit keys, 1536 qbits would be required and for 512-bit key – 3072. Given the speed at which quantum computer are increasing in performance (and this is currently faster than Moore's Law), it may only be a matter of years before the most popular cryptographic algorithms surrender their strongholds. As such, now is the time for cryptography specialists to address this potential threat.

Not everything is as grim as it would seem – a number of asymmetric cryptography algorithms have already been developed that retain their cryptographic security even when facing quantum brute force searches with a sufficiently large number of qbits. Such algorithms are referred to as "post-quantum," and we have already discussed some of them – in particular, the Lamport signature, lattice-based cryptography, and isogenies of elliptic curves.

Generating an electronic signature on the basis of the Lamport algorithm entails the use of a cryptographic hash function and a random number generator. So 256 pairs of random numbers are created with each one being 256 bits long. This data set is 16 kilobytes in total and will serve as the secret key. Each of the 256-bit pairs is hashed, and these 512 hashes jointly comprise the public key. Then, the electronic signature is generated on the basis of the secret key for the message to be sent. As you know, before electronically signing a message, it must first be hashed. Then, an electronic signature is generated, whereby for each bit value (zero or one) in the message hash, either the first or the second number is selected from the secret key pair corresponding to the sequence number of the bit in the hash.

This algorithm's cryptographic strength depends on the type of hash function used. Given that the hashing procedure is entirely non-reversible and that a significant amount of data (256 pairs) is hashed, not even a quantum computer is able to solve the problem of determining a private key from a public one. Yet, this algorithm also has its flaws. First of all, the keys are rather large (up to 16 kilobytes). Secondly, when using this algorithm to generate an electronic signature, half of the secret key actually enters the public domain. For this reason, it is not advised to use a signature based on one key more than a single time, which also poses considerable inconveniences for designing systems based on this algorithm.

The next algorithm which is also considered quantum-proof is the so-called "lattice-based cryptography." In mathematics, a lattice is a periodic network of points in an n-dimensional coordinate system, where n number of "basis vectors" is given which create the lattice. Here is a simple example of a lattice for a rectangular coordinate system with two given basis vectors:

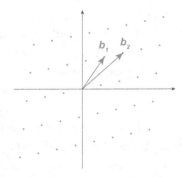

A difficult problem to calculate in this algorithm is the shortest vector problem (SVP), the shortest vector for given basis vectors which provides a significant increase in the dimension of the space n. If we consider an ordinary flat two-dimensional lattice, then it is not difficult for a person to visually identify the point closest to the given lattice node. However, if a computer is charged with this task, it will rely on elaborate mathematical computations. Moreover, once you begin to increase the number of spatial dimensions, the computations will quickly assume magnificent degrees of complexity. Modern theory holds that this currently exceeds the capacity of a quantum computer. However, of the algorithms using lattice-based cryptography, only the encryption itself seems to be free of vulnerabilities. The digital signature was subject to an attack in 1999 and a modified version thereof in 2006. Mathematicians are currently working on the further development of the digital signature algorithm in order solve this issue and provide the industry with a new, more advanced standard of cryptographic security.

Finally, we will consider what is perhaps the most promising algorithm at the moment – the use of cryptography based on the isogenies of elliptic curves. Isogeny is a method for mapping a point belonging to one elliptic curve to a point on another curve of the same type. The point transformation algorithm represents the ratio between two polynomials for each of the coordinates of a point on the x and y axes. If it is considered mathematically conceivable to obtain such a map, then these two curves will be isogenic with respect to one another. For each of the curves, we can calculate a "j-invariant," which is something like the "classifier" of an elliptic curve and given as a regular number. To calculate the j-invariant, the coefficients from the elliptic curve equation are used. By applying different values of coefficients, one can calculate a set of invariants which are then displayed as a graph. In the resulting graph, the invariants become its vertices, and the edges of the graph connect those invariants with isogenic curves which are isogenic to one another. Actually, finding paths in the graph between the vertices or, in other words, calculating the isogeny between different elliptic curves is the complex computational task upon which this cryptographic algorithm is built. Structures constructed on the basis of successively superimposed graphs of elliptic curves yield very beautiful geometric objects, such as the intricate "isogeny star" shown in the figure:

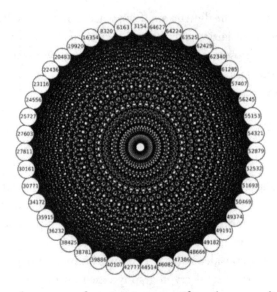

Obviously, the use of isogenies significantly complicates elliptic cryptography. If in the classical version we deal with only one elliptic curve, then in the case of isogenies, we deal with their whole family, which adds an additional degree of complexity to solving the problem. Even a quantum computer can't solve the problem in sub-exponential time, which is indicative of the algorithm's exceptional level of cryptographic security – it can truly be considered "post-quantum." At present, this algorithm is likely the most suitable foundation for blockchain projects which aim to ensure maximum data security for their users. In light of the rapidly developing quantum computing industry, this problem is assuming unquestionable relevance.

Game theory and blockchain

When we considered decentralization as a means of management, we outlined the issue of complexity in interaction among subjects with equal authorizations in systems where there is no center for consolidation and administration. And indeed, what would be the most efficient way for equal participants in a system to reach joint decisions which are satisfactory for essentially everyone, if not absolutely everyone? Clearly, there must be some procedurally conditioned form of public consent that allows decisions to be made in a manner which is binding on the entire community. At the same time, it should not create irresolvable conflicts that lead to the demise of the system as a whole. This set of measures is called the formation of rules for reaching consensus – i.e. unanimity of opinion among stakeholders when making decisions with system-wide implications without costly direct voting procedures (in terms of resources).

The word "game" can be used to describe the matrix of the system participants' endeavors to obtain personal or public benefit, while overcoming the overt or covert resistance of other participants with opposing interests. Naturally, to reach these individual aims, each of the participants implements some sort of strategy conceived with the aim of achieving maximum effect in solving the concrete tasks. In mathematics, there is a special discipline devoted to the study of optimal strategies in games. It is called "game theory," and we will consider its individual elements, as they are an important link in the construction of blockchain systems, which are almost always decentralized, and the hierarchy among its participants is flat. The primary issue is what methods are best for establishing consensus among the network nodes when creating a chain of blocks as well as sets of transactions therein. However, we will delve into that topic in greater detail in a little bit. First, let's establish some conceptual framework for what constitutes an effective or ineffective strategy for achieving general consent.

A strategy's effectiveness is inseparably tied to the notion of the participants' rational behavior. For proof that collaboration between the participants of the "game" is not always a given – even if it is in keeping with their common interests – consider the well-known "prisoner's dilemma." It was introduced in 1950 by American mathematicians Merrill Flood and Melvin Dresher. Nearly simultaneously, two criminals are thrown into prison for the same crime. In the reasonable assumption of possible collusion between the two criminals, the police decide to isolate them from each other and then offers each of them identical terms of cooperation with the investigation. More precisely, each prisoner is offered the opportunity to testify against the other in exchange for immediate release. Similarly, it is assumed that if the second prisoner does not cooperate with the police, they will receive the maximum sentence in prison. If both refuse to cooperate, each will get a minimum sentence. If they are both convicted, they will both receive an average sentence. Given that the prisoners are kept in isolation, they are not aware of one another's decision. So, what type of strategy is the most effective for each prisoner?

The dilemma of this situation arises from the fact that considering each prisoner individually and considering their common fate yields different optimal strategies which stand in diametric opposition to one another. For the first prisoner it is more expedient to make the other guy the scapegoat, and then they have a chance to immediately get out of prison. Yet, it is more prudent for the two prisoners as a group to remain silent, since the total sentence for both will be the smallest out of all possible outcomes. In other words, if both subjects individually behave in a rational manner, then collectively the result is an irrational decision. To a certain extent, this situation illustrates the complexity of the problems studied by game theory when one participant tries to maximize their own interest at the expense of the overall benefit. In blockchain systems, this practice is implemented as evidenced by the following example.

Let us assume that in a decentralized system that stores digital assets with an equivalent monetary value – e.g. cryptocurrencies – a node was discovered, which by means of various unscrupulous practices could impose an artificial transaction on the entire network whereby the given node acquires ownership of a tremendous number of digital coins. Question: who will benefit from this action? Some people would think that the attacker wins because their actions made them personally richer. The unquestionable losers were the former owners of the assets who lost them as a result of the attack on the network and on their personal accounts. The other system participants remained unaffected as they retained their own assets which the malicious node did not manage to reach. However, these conclusions are quite superficial. With his or her attack on the network, the hacker actually did something irreparable in that they undermined the overall credibility of the network as a whole – i.e. to its concept of security, cryptographic invulnerability, and consensus protocol.

This means an instant devaluation of all valuable assets belonging to the given network and having a monetary or even stock valuation. This also extends to the criminally obtained assets of the hacker. For this reason, their actions go from being personally expedient to collectively worthless. The network collapses and ceases to exist. In this situation, there are no winners: there are only losers.

- This example poignantly illustrates the importance of the consensus protocol in decentralized systems. Its role is no less important than that of the cryptographic strength of the data encryption algorithms employed in the system. What methods can be used in blockchain projects to obtain consensus? One of the most popular is the consensus based on the "Byzantine Generals Problem." Fast forward to the late Middle Ages, when the Byzantine Empire was already waning. Imagine that Byzantium is at war and the Emperor tasked a number of armies with capturing an enemy city and each of these armies is headed by a general. One would presume that generals are military people not alien to ideas of loyalty and honor, but in the Byzantium of that period, such qualities were in scarce supply among military leaders. For this reason, with some degree of probability, any one of these generals could be bribed by the enemy – i.e. become a traitor. Depending on the degree of their loyalty, each individual general could directly follow the order received from on high, or they could carry out the very opposite, thereby contributing to the empire's military defeat. Now back to mathematics, let's consider the possible outcome scenarios. True to their orders, the loyal generals lead their armies together to attack the city, and the city is taken: the war is won. Clearly, this is the best outcome for Byzantium.
- True to their orders, the loyal generals retreat in unison, whereby the city is not taken, but all the armies are saved for future battles. This outcome can be considered intermediate.
- Following their orders, the loyal generals attack, but rather than attacking, the traitor generals begin to retreat, resulting in all the armies being destroyed by the enemy and Byzantium losing the war itself. This is the worst possible scenario.

Occasionally, the task can be additionally complicated by the presence of a commander-in-chief, who has the authority to give orders to subordinate generals. The crux of the complication is that the commander-in-chief can also be a traitor. As such, they will give different generals conflicting orders in order to be certain of the worst possible outcome for Byzantium. In this case, the most effective behavior for all the generals would be a strategy of completely ignoring the orders of the commander-in-chief. Leaving aside questions of military discipline, let us focus on how best to deal with such a scenario. It is clear that if each general acts in keeping with their discretion (presuming equal probability of attacking or retreating), the likelihood of a satisfactory or even intermediate outcome for Byzantium is extremely small. The only optimal solution in this situation would be a direct exchange of information between the generals.

The generals may share a variety of different information – e.g. providing information on the size of each of the armies or simply indicating their intention to attack or retreat. The important thing is that each of the generals (let's assume that their number is n) sends all the other generals their own information and receives in return n-1 sets of similar information. However, that's not all. As such, each general has at their disposal a certain amount of information received via direct communication with all the other generals. Moreover, they can both relay the information received to all the generals and receive similar sets of data from others. This would require that each general has not only the information that they received directly from each of the other generals, but also the big picture of how the information was communicated – i.e. "which general reported what to whom." However, we account for the possibility that one or even more generals may be traitors and thus deliberately distort the information conveyed. Nonetheless, it is always possible to cross-check what each particular general has reported to the other generals and examine it for discrepancies. The data obtained make it possible to identify the share of generals who are disloyal and approximate their overall number. Mathematical proofs have demonstrated that in cases where at least two-thirds of the nodes are loyal, the system is considered stable and consensus can be reached. Otherwise, the system's viability is compromised and the participants' confidence lost.

The principle of resistance to the "Byzantine fault" is a classic problem from game theory which represents an important security concern in achieving consensus in blockchain projects. Each node in the system must strictly follow the system rules set forth in the form of algorithmic logic of the node software. However, almost all the software in blockchain projects is provided as open-source code that each node can modify at will so as to vie for preferences to which it would not otherwise be entitled. However, even if a single node (or a group of nodes) introduces some changes without the authorization of the network, it would require a relatively large number of nodes for the attack to be successful. Otherwise, the rest of the network will reject any information from the violators because the information will not comply with the general rules which govern the majority. This captures the very essence of consensus which is critical for administration in decentralized systems. System integrity is violated if the number of "dissident" nodes begins to exceed the critical mass, after which there is a split of the network called a "fork." The nodes with different rules of consensus form separate networks, which from the moment of splitting become autonomous and thus different projects, albeit with similar technology (at least initially). At a later point, we will revisit the concept of the "fork" as an important phenomenon in the blockchain industry.

In order to illustrate how consensus functions in blockchain environments with specific examples, we first need to familiarize ourselves with the structure of blocks and transactions as well as examine the principles responsible for forming blocks and chains. In the previous chapters, we examined all the important elements of the blockchain technology separately and now we can start to piece our pieces of knowledge together like a hamburger where all of the ingredients have been cut, measured, and laid out in advance in a restaurant kitchen. We will offer it for consumption to the guests invited to the feast, whose opening festivities ran somewhat over for purely technical reasons.

Blocks and their structure

In the description of the general principles of building the blockchain structure, the architecture of a decentralized database was compared to an accounting ledger in which the pages were blocks where financial transactions were recorded. The point was made separately that these "pages" are arranged in a strict sequence that cannot be changed because they are firmly linked to one other by special "cryptographic locks." Now that we have familiarized ourselves with the basic technological elements of blockchain networks, including cryptography, we can delve deeper into how the integrity of the block structure is maintained and what impact this has on the overall security of information storage in distributed systems. It should come as no surprise that each blockchain system individually has its own structural design features, and when the time comes for us to study the most popular implementations of various projects, we will identify and carefully examine these features. That said, nearly all systems built on blockchain technology have common principles of how the structure and its elements are formed. For this reason, it makes sense to consider them in the context of the general description; indeed, in most practical cases, the degree of technological similarity is quite high from one project to another, without significant differences.

The idea of storing information in the form of connected lists had existed for quite some time – in fact, it predates by far computer technologies. To be more precise, the idea can be traced back 4000 years ago to the Inca civilization and its predecessors around the 3rd millennium BCE. We are talking about a way to store information in the form of the "khipu" – threads intricately strung on a single rope base and connected to one other depending on the context of the recorded information. Each thread could have its own color code, as well as special knots, whose shape and number were important markers which determined the values and types of information stored. By tracing each strand from beginning to end, you could determine the entire path of data chain formation – from the base rope to the end of the branch. The total number of threads in a single khipu could reach 2500. As the ruling class of the Central Andean tribes, the Incas could take into account, with the help of the khipu, all the necessary resources under their control – troops, food supplies, population, and the amount of taxes payable.

The Spanish conquistadors who arrived in the first half of the 16th century did not immediately grasp the utilitarian purpose of these strange knot-and-rope devices, which aided the Incas in ruling their empire. Breaking the established order of government meant that the Spaniards had to impose European principles of writing and data accounting throughout the conquered territories. The khipu were completely disbanded, and only at the beginning of the 19th century did scientists undertake somewhat systematic study of the device. They managed to decipher a lot of the information contained in the surviving khipu. Once they grasped the basic principles underlying such an accounting system, scientists were astonished that such an ancient civilization being isolated from the more progressive world, was able to find such an efficient way of compactly recording and storing data which obeyed the logic of connecting information blocks.

In the second half of the 20th century, when information technologies began their gradual global conquest, it became necessary to create various forms of recording and storing information. One of these forms was linked lists which are special data structures that each contained not only data as such, but also special links to similar – both preceding and subsequent – structures. In this way, it became possible to disregard the natural order of storing data on various media and be guided by information logistics, the principle of which was laid down in a set of internal links between the blocks. Depending on the logic of solving the given tasks, the forms of data lists in most cases could be singly linked (unidirectional) or two-linked (bidirectional). Also, both forms of lists could have a circular structure, when the last element refers to the first or vice-versa. A simple example of a singly linked list is shown in the figure:

Actually, in its classical form, the blockchain is a singly linked list, when each next block in the system refers to the previous one. The question is what "refers" means: how is this technologically implemented, and, most importantly, what purpose does it serve? The answer is simple: it is done to maintain the integrity of the database. The block consists of two main parts – a header containing service information and a list of transactions for the transfer of digital assets between system participants or the simple recording of facts. This is all expressed as a set of data that can be displayed as a standard-length hash. After calculating the hash of the header data, we fix the state of the entire block, and any interference with its integrity will immediately lead to a fundamental change in the total hash. What if each new block were to contain a hash of the data of the previous block as one of the elements in its header? In this case, it turns out that by hashing the data of one header, we automatically include the hash of the header of the previous block, and thus get the form of a chain of blocks. We have already seen that any small change in the pre-image changes its hash beyond recognition. It thus follows that if we tamper with any bit of data from any of the blocks in the middle of the chain, all the hashes of the subsequent blocks will also be recalculated. In other words, the data will change throughout the whole chain.

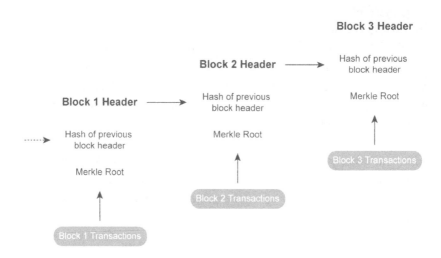

What does the connected structure of blocks tell us in the first place? It tells us that the blockchain is a system where information can only be added, but not altered or deleted. That said, information can only be added in the form of new blocks and, moreover, only at the end of the chain. While this does introduce a certain inconvenience as concerns management of the information placed on the blockchain, it also lays the framework for exceptionally secure distributed data storage. After all, each system participant receives a copy of the entire database of blocks along with the ability to make record any information on the blockchain. Yet, any changes made in violation of the system rules will not be accepted by the other network members. Moreover, compliance with the rules is checked by the system participants in a strictly mathematical manner, thus rendering it entirely impossible to feed them distorted information. Algorithms for checking the information contained in the blocks will immediately signal a violation of the data integrity, and the block in question will be considered unacceptable for the entire network.

That's not all: since data can only be added but never deleted – even if it eventually loses its relevance – the total base is in a perpetual state of growth from the moment when the first block is created. Its size depends on different parameters, such as the amount of time required to make new blocks, the number of transactions contained therein, the size of the transactions themselves. Depending on these parameters and the age of the database, within just a few years of active operation, it can reach a size of hundreds of gigabytes of information which is constantly copied and synchronized between the system participants. Developers in mainstream systems would be well advised to find a solution for optimizing the size of the database in the blockchain so as to avoid further obstacles to the development of this promising technology. For what it's worth, proposals have been put forth for solving this problem, and we will touch on them in the section devoted to scaling of the blockchain technology.

Let's take a look at the structure of the block header in greater detail to understand what kind of service information it contains. Admittedly, the various implementations of blockchain technology always use different block structures, but nearly all of the projects have a number of common elements that appear in one form or another. Generally speaking, the first item in any block is its sequence number. The very first block is called the "genesis" block, and it differs from the others in that it does not contain a reference to the previous block because no such block exists. Usually, a block contains information about its version number, which can be required if the block structure subsequently undergoes changes, and depending on the version number, software algorithms will have to process them differently. Next, as noted earlier, the header contains a hash of the previous block header to maintain the data integrity of the entire chain.

Another important element of the header is the time when the block was created. It is written as a number equal to the number of seconds that have elapsed since January 1, 1970 – a format adopted by multiuser and multitasking operating systems such as Unix and other compatible operating systems. As a side note, it's worth mentioning that this number is quite large, and in a couple of decades we will likely see an overflow of the 32-bit memory cell typically usually allocated for the variables which store this value in various software. If the developers of these programs do not make the corrections necessary to increase the size of the variable that stores the time values to 64 bits, then on January 19, 2038, mass software failures can occur worldwide. The explanation for this is that when executing programs, the specific construction of computer architecture will render values of this number which will then be interpreted as being negative, thus triggering a host of algorithmic consequences.

Finally, let's move on to the part of the header devoted to the transactions contained in the block. One of the values in the header is the number of transactions in the block, but the second value is mysteriously called the "Merkle root." In all reality, this is just the combined hash of all the transactions in a given block, calculated in a certain way. In 1979, American cryptographer Ralph Merkle patented an algorithm for calculating the resulting hash for a data set constructed as a binary tree:

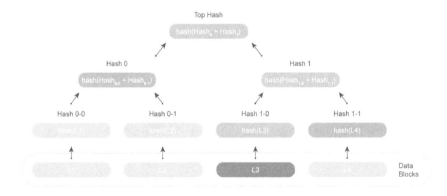

According to the logic of Merkle's algorithm, all transactions in a block are divided into pairs, hashed, and their hashes are summed together. If there was an odd total number of transactions, then the hash of the last transaction (i.e. the one lacking a pair) is simply doubled. At the next level of the "tree," the number of hashes is two times smaller than one step prior and this number must be even. Again, the hashes are divided into pairs, these pairs are added, and so on, until only one finite number remains. As a result, the resulting or root hash is formed at the top of the tree, which is called the "Merkle root" and is actually a single aggregate print of all the transactions of the block. It stands to reason that if you change any of the transactions in the block, all the hashes of the Merkle tree are immediately recalculated again and the resulting hash will also change, which will also serve as a marker of the attempt to interfere with the block data. Thus, the Merkle root value is the "representative" of the transactional part of the block in its own header. As it is "hashed" to the general header data and thus indirectly included in the header of the next block, the Merkle root offers further guarantee of the immutability of transactions previously recorded in the blockchain.

In addition to the parameters of the block structure described above, it may also contain elements related to the direct acquisition of the right to create a block and protect it from possible future changes. We are speaking here of creating new blocks in proof-of-work (PoW) systems. Nonetheless, it is still a bit premature to dive into that topic, so let's first take a look at the structure of transactions and the principles of maintaining balances in blockchain systems.

Transactions and balances

Nearly everyone has experience dealing with traditional banks: opening accounts, making payments from one current account to another, receiving funds to your account. In the last couple of decades, "Bank–Client" systems have become commonplace, allowing you to manage your accounts via the internet. Despite the external differences in such systems (primarily in terms of the interface design), their functionality is more or less the same for all financial institutions which offer such services. In most cases, to access your funds via the internet, you must go through a two-factor identification procedure. First, the user enters the usual (static) password, and then the system asks for a special one-time code, which can either be generated by a special device or received by SMS or email. This prevents unauthorized access to the client's account, whose data is stored on the bank's servers – i.e. in a centralized manner. If the bank's servers for some reason do not work (e.g. due to maintenance), access to the account will be blocked until the system returns to normal operation.

Upon gaining access to their account, the client can check their balance and then transfer funds from this account by using a system which generates one-time passwords, as required by the security rules of accessing data. Each account has its own number generated in keeping with certain rules and standards laid down by either the bank itself or the governmental body relevant for the particular bank. When wiring payments to other accounts, the bank typically charges a commission for its services, the amount of which is determined depending on the bank's business costs, established profit margins, and the competitive situation in the banking market. Obviously, in order for the customer to make or receive payments, the bank must first open a current account and give them the details of access to the online bank; otherwise, no incoming or outgoing transfers are possible.

In blockchain systems, everything is set up quite differently. First, there are no banks or other centralized authorities monitoring the accounts and payments made to or from such. Secondly, no accounts are created in advance, and no one in particular is charged with maintaining the balances on them. At first glance, it seems a little strange, but this is what sets apart the payment system projects built on the basis of blockchain technology. In order to become a member of the system, the user needs to generate a pair of keys

– private and public – via the asymmetric cryptography algorithm relevant in the given blockchain environment. The keys in a pair are always inseparably connected to one another – the private one can be generated randomly, and the public one is calculated mathematically from it. However, the system software performs all of this automatically at the request of the user who merely needs to press the appropriate button in the client program interface. In this way, the user obtains their own account in the system, although it would be more accurate to call it an address. Moreover, this address is actually a modification of the public key which was processed during creation by several procedures of hashing and special character encoding. This is done not only to streamline the visual presentation of the address, but also to further complicate the task of restoring the associated private key, since one-way hash functions – not to mention when applied several times in a row – only complicate any attempts to crack the address of the blockchain system.

It's worth remembering that these networks are decentralized, so any actions performed by the user are not carried out on some remote server, but rather directly on the user's computer or mobile device, which is also where all the necessary keys (including private ones) are stored In contrast to a traditional bank, the issues of keeping personal information secret are now left to the client. If they lose the secret key, they will automatically lose access to the assets held at the address generated from this secret key. On the internet, you can find an endless number of tales about failed cryptocurrency millionaires who lost their private keys and, therewith, millions held in digital assets. Given the serious nature of this issue, a separate chapter will be devoted to the secure storage of cryptoassets.

Once the user has an address in the some blockchain system, let's break down the process of how they can receive digital assets to their own address and then transfer them to other addresses. Again, it makes sense to return to the analogy with the ledger which consists of pages listing financial transactions: from whom, to whom, how much, and for what. Let's imagine a business environment where there are multiple participants who are constantly exchanging goods, services, and money. Moreover, all of the exchange-related exchanges are recorded in a special book. When one of the participants wants to transfer a certain amount to another, they first need to prove that they possess the requisite funds. To this end, the only viable option is to indicate previous incoming transactions credited to this participant – i.e. refer to them as proof of ownership of certain assets. Furthermore, if no single transaction is sufficient to demonstrate sufficient funds for the outgoing payment, reference can be made to several transactions.

When a bank transfers money from one account to another, it performs the following three operations: subtracts the amount for transfer and the transfer fee from the sender's account and adds the appropriate amount to the recipient's account. The bank retains the fee as payment for the completed intermediary service. In blockchain systems, there are no intermediaries, just as no funds are physically deducted or added. The owner of the assets simply indicates the addresses of one or more recipients in the transaction which induces the creation of further links. As such, the transaction represents a set of links to the funds received at the payer's address as well as a set of links to the addresses of the recipients of their payments. The blockchain environment functions with the concepts of "inputs" and "outputs" for such transactions. A rule stipulates that the sum of all funds in "outputs" must be equal to the amount of funds in "inputs." If the owner of the address does not need to employ the entirety of the funds on the "inputs" involved in the transaction, they generate an additional "output" in the form of change for themselves to maintain an equal balance of "inputs" and "outputs." Clearly, the "output" for the sender will be the "input" for the recipient who will in turn be able to make reference to it when they make their own outgoing payments.

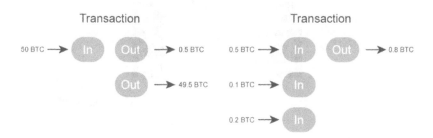

What conclusions can we draw from the description of this model? First, if you start from the first block (i.e. the genesis block) of the database and analyze all the "inputs" to a specific address and all the "outputs" from it, you can easily identify how much the owner of this address has left in unspent "outputs." This is the account balance. In other words, no balance is stored anywhere per se, but rather it is simply calculated as the sum of all unspent "outputs." Second, by indicating an "output" to a particular address, the sender assumes that there is a system member with a private key to that address. Otherwise, if you incorrectly enter the recipient's address, the system will nonetheless accept the transaction making reference to it, but the funds of this outgoing transaction will be permanently lost and excluded from circulation. This owes to the fact that transactions placed in a block which have passed the consensus procedure and are included in the overall block chain can never be changed in the future. Some projects, such as Bitcoin, offer some measure of built-in protection against errors by converting the address in hexadecimal format to alphanumeric format, adding its checksum to the end of the received address. When the recipient's address is entered in the appropriate field of the funds transfer form, in the event of an error in the calculation and comparison of the checksum, the system will issue a warning. It is also quite common for the address to be represented as a QR code, so that the sender can scan it with their mobile phone and automatically convert it into the correct set of letters and numbers comprising the recipient's address.

This gives rise to the question: when transferring funds, can a system member make reference to "inputs" which do not actually belong to him, and how can this be checked? In fact, in order to legitimately refer to "inputs," in the link you must specify your public key and your digital electronic signature generated on the basis of the private key associated with the owner's address. With the help of digital signature verification algorithms, any member of the system can make sure that the reference to the "inputs" is indeed legitimate. Moreover, in the event of a validation error, this transaction is simply ignored and not included in the block by the node that creates it for the network.

Such systems of generating transactions and maintaining balances is called the unspent transaction outputs (UTXO). As stated above, in order to calculate the balance associated with a specific address in the system, you must find and check all the associated "inputs" and "outputs" starting from the genesis block. An advantage of this method is that you do not need to separately store the status of balances and constantly update them, thus saving free space on the media. A disadvantage is the time constantly spent on the calculating the balance, especially if the base of blocks has grown significantly. For this reason, a number of projects still keep special "up-to-date" databases that contain, inter alia, data on address balances, and this information can be quickly fetched from the databases.

Now let's consider what additional service information can be placed in the transaction. First, there is a transaction identifier with a unique number that cannot be repeated. It is derived from the hash of the transaction itself because as we have seen, cryptographically strong hash functions have a very low probability of getting a collision (i.e. the same hash for different pre-images). Second, similar to the way it is done in the headers of the blocks themselves, the hash of the previous transaction in the given block is usually placed in the body of the transaction. The presence of this information in every transaction serves the same purpose: to maintain the integrity of data storage and protect it from unauthorized changes. Also, when describing the references to the "inputs," the public key of the address and the electronic signature are indicated, which proves that the author of the transaction has a private key from this pair.

In wrapping up the general description of transactions, I should mention a bit about the commission. Various blockchain projects charge a fee for transactions, although there are some projects where all transactions are free of charge. The purpose of the fee is to provide monetary motivation for the nodes that create blocks: they retain it for themselves in addition to the main remuneration for actually creating the block. In the chapter on "mining," we will revisit this process in greater detail, so for now we will only mention that the fees in blockchain systems, as a rule, are not fixed and the individual setting up the transaction decides what size of fee to pay. However, if this fee is not competitively set (i.e. too low or even zero), the transaction may receive a low priority when forming new blocks and will be included in some of them with a large time delay. As for how the fee amount is shown in the body in the transaction, the approach used aims to maximize usability in the organization of data storage. In reality, no transaction fee is directly specified in the transactions; instead, it is calculated it as the difference between the sum of all "inputs" and "outputs," including the "change" minus the fee to be paid.

The chapter on transactions and balances concludes the first section of the book, which contains a description of the general principles underlying the vast majority of projects based on blockchain technology. The next section will concentrate on the most popular practical implementations built on the distributed ledger technology.

Part II

Practical implementations

Background of the Bitcoin project

Description of any large-scale phenomenon usually starts with its first appearance and then moves on to its further development. Yet, before we could undertake a full-fledged narration of blockchain's history, we needed to acquaint ourselves with a number of scientific and technological aspects. Otherwise, the inexperienced reader would inevitably encounter difficulties in understanding what exactly has been invented and why this technological novelty has such significance.

The past few decades have seen a fair number of attempts to conceive technologically secure digital money. All of the projects that popped up in this domain were based on one or more technologies that later formed an integral part of the blockchain concept. However, until the appearance of the Bitcoin network, no single project had managed to combine all the necessary components so as to obtain a finished, secure, and ultimately elegant solution to the problem of creating a decentralized digital currency. For now, let's look at the actual history of the first attempts to develop a form of electronic money.

In 1976, still in the pre-internet era, the famous Austrian economist Friedrich August von Hayek presented his book entitled *The Denationalization of Money*. It contained serious arguments regarding the possible elimination of the state monopoly in the management of issuing currency, including proposals for the creation of competitive financial systems. Von Hayek also wrote about the possible negative consequences of national governments abusing public trust. To a significant extent, these warnings did indeed materialize when the financial world began to be buffeted by systemic crises generated by the irresponsible policy of large banks and financial regulators of a number of states. Von Hayek's ideas resonated with some enthusiastic cryptographers who began to think seriously about designing independent electronic money systems. Above all, they were interested in the possibility of decentralizing and, simultaneously, rendering the circulation of money anonymous by ridding the system of intermediaries, which in most cases are under strict state control.

In 1982, the American cryptographer David Chaum published a paper entitled "Blind signatures for untraceable payments" as an extension of his research in the field of encrypted communications. We have already discussed the concept of blind signatures, so the reader should already a general notion of how they function. It was on the basis of this form of e-signature that Chaum subsequently created the first electronic cash system, which he called eCash. This project used "blind digital signature" technology to authorize and verify digital banknotes exchanged by counterparties. At the same time, the authorizing party played the role of the bank – a centralized service with the primary function of protecting the system from the threat of repeat expenditure of the digital money. However, such centralization could potentially lead to customer balances being falsified, if the system owners wished to do so. Nonetheless, it was the first project to use asymmetric cryptography algorithms to create an electronic payment system.

To ensure the operation of the eCash project, the company DigiCash was registered in the Netherlands in 1990, which cooperated from 1990–1995 with banks and large payment systems, including such as VISA. Even Microsoft did not remain a passive onlooker and tried to integrate this project into Windows 95, which at that time was its most cutting edge and, in many ways, a revolutionary operating system. The idea was that the presence of interest from such serious partners would secure excellent prospects of development for DigiCash. However, miscalculations in Chaum's business strategy brought the company to bankruptcy in 1998, after which its assets were sold and the project was shut down.

Around that same time, Wei Dai, a computer engineer and graduate of the University of Washington, put forth a paper describing the B-money project, which the author defined as a distributed and anonymous electronic money system. This project enabled the concept of transferring digital cash between owners of asymmetric cryptography keys in roughly the same manner as described in the chapter dedicated to transactions and balances in the blockchain. Moreover, a B-money transaction was generated via the transfer of digital assets to the public key of the recipient which plays the role of an address or account and was secured by the sender's electronic signature generated with their private key. As in the blockchain, it was assumed that both the sender and the recipient always control their private keys and can thus transfer digital money to each other, while simultaneously providing mathematical proof of their respective ownership right. Regrettably, the concept of B-money was not implemented as a project, but rather went down in history in purely descriptive terms, although it would ultimately have a significant impact on the further evolution of digital payment systems.

In general, 1998 was a year of monumental events in the global financial industry. Originating in Asia, the global financial crisis swept across the globe like a hurricane and wreaked significant economic damage in several developing countries. This compelled many to ponder the extent to which the existing global financial system – with its significant degree of centralization – is prone to economic crises. The causes that gave rise to them stemmed from either excessive governmental regulation of the national economies or plain-and-simple incompetence on the part of those heading large financial institutions – moreover, both commercial and state-owned structures, including central banks. Perhaps, this was when the ideas of decentralized monetary circulation began to emerge which made it possible to avoid extreme dependence on the situational decisions of the particular individuals to whom fate has entrusted political and economic power in their states. As a result, subsequent projects relating to the decentralization of payment processes incorporated all the effective methods previously developed in this sector of the industry. In this way, the industry inched ever closer to creating a solution which would unleash a veritable revolution in the system of monetary relations.

A further example of such was the BitGold project developed in the same year – despite not being publicly presented until 2005 – by an American scientist of Hungarian origin Nick Szabo, a specialist in the fields of cryptography, computer science, and law. In addition to asymmetric cryptography, his system included an interesting element that would later play a major role in blockchain technology – namely the need for system users to solve complex computational problems in order to constitute the issue of electronic money. The task was to find hashes of a specially given type, where the end result was to find a data string starting with a certain number of bits with a value of zero. Given that the hash function yields a result which is algorithmically dependent, yet visually unpredictable, you need to sort through a large number of different source pre-images in order to obtain – in a perfectly random manner – the hash that will satisfy the conditions of the problem. In the given case, it needs to contain the required number of zero characters at the beginning of the data string.

Nick Szabo borrowed this technique to form a complex task from the author of the Hashcash project Adam Beck, who in 1997 used a similar algorithm in a system for counteracting mass email newsletters. Beck's project also required the calculation of a hash when sending each letter, where the first 20 bits of the result needed to be zeros. Computationally speaking, the task itself was simple and in terms of search options was limited to a maximum of 2^{20} options (i.e. approximately 1 million) which a standard computer could solve in a matter of seconds. However, a similar task had to be performed for each letter sent, and if the number of recipients in the mailing list was significant, the amount of time spent on calculations increased proportionally. The result of calculations was added to the service information accompanying each email, after which the recipient's computer could readily verify its "validity" by checking for the required number of leading zeros. This greatly simplified the work of spam filters in classifying the received email message.

On an anecdotal note, Szabo deliberately placed the word "gold" in the project name – the author wanted to liken the concept of computationally complex digital money with gold which is not so easily found, mined, or replicated. To obtain an ingot of gold or jewelry made of gold can be obtained only by serious efforts – first by the work of geologists and miners, then by foundry workers and finally by jewelers. The value of gold is determined by the combination of its rarity, unique chemical properties, and the labor required for extraction and processing. Another important factor for the value is the balance of supply and demand of this metal in the global market. Nonetheless, the primary determining factor for the value of gold is that the fact of owning it attests to the phenomenal amount of work required to obtain it.

In 1999, a paper authored by cryptographers Marcus Jacobson and Ari Jewels first introduced the concept of proof-of-work. This term refers to solving the cryptographic problem of finding a secret initial pre-image with a hash which satisfies certain complexity requirements. Moreover, any other member of the network that receives this pre-image could easily verify its validity by running the hashing procedure. This provided unambiguous proof that the node claiming credit for such had indeed carried out the complex computational work.

In his project BitGold, Nick Szabo truly came very close to solving the problem of creating secure digital money by using most of the technologies which had been previously developed. However, there was a vulnerability in his system, which is called the "Sybil Attack" – when in a distributed network, a particular node can infiltrate the environment of a number of other nodes controlled by attackers. Nodes which fall victim to these attacks will then be fed false information about network transactions and their own transactions sent to the network can be modified by the attacking nodes. In addition, there were other problems that ultimately prevented Szabo from putting his project into practice. For example, he failed to constructively address the issue of inflation of digital money, which would inevitably accompany the gradual increase in the computing power of network nodes.

Nevertheless, those who created these systems did not labor in vain. Only a short time later, these principles would be reflected in a document that was presented to the world by an author whose name was entirely unknown at that time. Even today, very few have heard of him or her. We are talking about someone whose existence remains a mystery to this very day. We are talking about the creator of the blockchain technology and Bitcoin – the first project built on it. Name of this creator – Satoshi Nakamoto, who on October 31, 2008 presented to the cryptographic community an article describing the principles of his revolutionary project, which received worldwide fame after some time. Who is this Satoshi Nakamoto and how did his project of distributed digital money differ from similar ones previously proposed by other experts in the field of asymmetric cryptography?

Mastermind behind Bitcoin

As the Bitcoin project came into public renown, many wondered: who is Satoshi Nakamoto? Is there actually person with such a name, or are we dealing only with an exotic pseudonym? Writing the name "Satoshi Nakamoto" in Japanese requires the use of three characters. "Satoshi" means "resourceful," "wise," "clear thinking." In the last name, "Naka" means "relationship," and "Moto" is "foundation" or "origin." Since the real Nakamoto did not leave a single technical description in Japanese, and all communications were conducted in impeccable English, it was concluded unequivocally that the enigmatic inventor comes from an English-speaking environment.

At some point, a few fastidious journalists managed to find a man living in the United States with the name Satoshi Nakamoto, but he stubbornly denied any involvement in the creation of Bitcoin. For what it's worth, no had insisted on his involvement. In fact, the man did not seem a very strong match for the profile of an individual actually capable of creating such a project. Moreover, he must be the owner of a significant cryptocurrency reserve, making him a billionaire and one of the richest people in the world. The man in question was an elderly Japanese American living in Temple City, California.

A graduate of the Physics Department of California Polytechnic University and fond of railway models, Dorian Satoshi Nakamoto clearly has legitimate mathematical abilities and even possesses programming skills. Nonetheless, he claims to have a rather weak grasp on cryptography and to have only learned of Bitcoin from the journalists who appeared on his doorstep. This, however, did not keep him from calling the police – just in case. In addition, he said that he had been unemployed for a long time and living on odd jobs such that his income had taken a heavy hit. In fact, his financial problems were so aggravated that he supposedly had even found himself forced to have the internet disconnected from his home. Ultimately, Nakamoto requested that "others respect my right to privacy and leave me alone," and even tried to sue several excessively intrusive journalists. However, he also expressed gratitude to the representatives of the crypto community for the moral and material support extended that was provided to him to a certain extent. This left many to conclude either that Mr. Nakamoto was very skillfully pretending to be innocent or that he was really telling the truth. In that case, finding the real creator of Bitcoin will take substantially more effort. Similarly, there could even be multiple creators – i.e. no single person, but a whole group of people – and this scenario could indeed be plausible.

If we assume that we are dealing with the pseudonym of a particular person, then one of the best candidates for the role of the cryptic founder of blockchain technology would be Nick Szabo, the author of BitGold. As you know, the principles of construction of both projects were quite similar, and Szabo stopped essentially one step short of the success demonstrated by Bitcoin. Moreover, it seems quite suspicious that in his description of the Bitcoin project Satoshi Nakamoto did not mention Nick Szabo among the many predecessors in the quest to create digital money although it was his project that bore the strongest resemblance to Nakamoto's creation. As for Szabo himself, he immediately and resolutely renounced all claims of authorship and took no further steps to change the existing state of affairs in this matter. At the same time, Szabo expressed satisfaction that his research in the field of cryptography and digital money had found such successful development in its practical application. However, when the Bitcoin project first appeared, Szabo seemingly did not notice it and did not provide any manner of comment, although the creation of decentralized digital money had veritably been his life's endeavor. In all fairness, Szabo substantially contributed to the creation of the blockchain technology and also introduced the concept of "smart contracts" which were first implemented in the Ethereum system and then in other blockchain platforms.

As for the question of searching for candidates for Bitcoin authorship, admittedly not all the candidates put forth by journalists or representatives of the crypto community denied these assumptions. In particular, in 2016, Australian scientist, programmer, and entrepreneur Craig Steven Wright claimed to have founded the Bitcoin project. However, he was never able to provide convincing evidence of his authorship – when he was asked to generate a digital electronic signature based on the private key used to sign the first Bitcoin transactions (undoubtedly owned by Satoshi Nakamoto), Wright refused to do so. For that, he was subjected to public censure by the blockchain community which accused him of outright imposture and deception. We will add also that shortly before Wright declared himself the author, his house in Sydney was raided by police in connection with suspicions of money laundering. After this, he seemingly decided to draw attention to himself in a similar – if exceptionally dubious – manner. In the view of several specialists, Wright's acquaintance with the technical side of the Bitcoin project is quite superficial, which decidedly does not bolster his authorship claim.

If you start perusing the articles dedicated to finding the Bitcoin creator, the inquiry ends up taking on a fantastic air – at one point or another, they have scrutinized, seemingly, nearly everyone. These assumptions have extended to many well-known figures in the IT industry. The list includes Bill Gates, the founder of Microsoft, and Steve Jobs, the founder of Apple, and even Elon Musk, one of the co-founders of the companies PayPal, Tesla, and Space X. All of them, of course, quickly denied any form of involvement in the creation of Bitcoin. Among the authoritative representatives of the crypto community, at one point or another, allegations of Bitcoin authorship were made of Gavin Andresen who founded the Bitcoin Foundation (a non-profit organization dedicated to the standardization, protection, and promotion of the use of Bitcoin worldwide) as well as of Charlie Lee who founded the Litecoin project, which used the Bitcoin code to offer an alternative to the Bitcoin project.

In fact, the list of potential candidates for the title of Bitcoin creator is so large that we simply cannot go through the entire list and look at each of the individuals in detail. As for Gavin Andersen specifically, he was in correspondence with the actual Satoshi Nakamoto for about two years, until the sudden disappearance of all types of communications in the spring of 2011. In the words of Nakamoto himself, he was "retiring to attend to more important matters." Throughout their communication, Andersen believed that he was dealing with a talented individual of Japanese origin with a strong level of English. However, having received from Nakamoto the software of the Bitcoin network client, Andersen and his colleagues had to rewrite about 70% of the code, as they considered it quite "sloppy." By the way, this factor led them to believe that Nakamoto created Bitcoin most likely alone, otherwise the code would not contain so many errors and would be more "legible." For some time after, Anderson considered Craig Wright to the person with whom he communicated as the author of Bitcoin before he realized his mistake, whereupon the question of authorship again became relevant.

Finally, the search for the real creator was undertaken by an authoritative body – the National Security Agency of the United States. Their in-house specialists conducted a linguistic analysis of all the texts attributed to Nakamoto, which he placed on various forums dedicated to the subjects of cryptography and the creation of digital means of payment. In their work, the analysts made use of "stylometry" which enabled them to study stylistic elements in the written texts by employing statistical analysis to gauge repetitions of various words. This method is also called "writer invariant" which reflects a quantitative characteristic of literary texts. Nakamoto's texts were compared with the texts of other authors, and the number of these samples bordered on the trillions. This resulted in a unique "digital fingerprint" of Nakamoto's texts which served as a unique identifier of his authorship. With access to a huge repository of electronic messages, chat logs, and the traffic archives of processing centers and data storage of corporations such as Google, Amazon, and Facebook, the NSA experts were able to compare the Nakamoto's "fingerprint" with data belonging to at least one billion people. We know that the data processing took about a month, and rumor has it that a positive search result was obtained which the NSA, however, continues to keep secret.

Why did this mysterious Satoshi Nakamoto decide to remain incognito? There is no clear answer to this question, and we can only speculate about the reasons that prompted him to do so. Did he do it out of natural modesty or was he motivated by personal security considerations, knowing that his invention could unleash a revolution in the world of business and social relationships? Did he anticipate that many national governments would be concerned with the problems of decentralization of money creation, anonymization of financial flows and, consequently, the possible loss of control over them? In any case, Satoshi Nakamoto disappeared and never again appeared on the internet or in any media. In the last message from him, in response to Andersen's offer to accept an invitation to meet with the CIA, Nakamoto wrote the following:

I hope that by talking to them directly, I will be able to answer all their questions and dispel their doubts. I want to try to convince them that Bitcoin is simply a means of payment which is more effective and independent from the actions of politicians. Not the omnipotent black market tool which they believe anarchists will use to fight the System.

Those fortunate enough to communicate directly with Nakamoto via the internet, noted his high education, as well as serious qualifications as an expert in cryptography and programming. In addition, Nakamoto's libertarian views were clearly evident, as well as his wariness towards state governments, taxes, banks, and persons associated with them. Perhaps by keeping his real name secret, Nakamoto hoped to protect Bitcoin from government interference, which could possibly seek to keep the project from ever seeing the light of day. In Nakamoto's own words, work on creating the Bitcoin concept took him at least seven years and he was convinced that he had finally solved the problem exceeded the capacities of his predecessors. In any case, it is time for us to consider the following questions in detail – what is the Bitcoin project and what is its technological structure?

How Bitcoin is set up

Admittedly, in previous chapters, our descriptions of the various methodologies, approaches, and technologies used to build projects on the blockchain were based on the principles of the Bitcoin project. Of course, ten years after its appearance, Bitcoin looks somewhat archaic in comparison with more modern blockchain projects. However, it was Bitcoin that laid the foundations for the subsequent evolution of blockchain technology. We will not repeat in detail the technological descriptions of the main methods used in the Bitcoin network given that we have already discussed these in an earlier portion of the book. Yet, at the same time, Bitcoin contains a number of additional features that we have not yet described. Now, we have the chance to dwell on those in greater detail.

First, let's try to understand how the addressing system is set up in the Bitcoin network. In order to get an address in the Bitcoin network, you must first generate a pair of keys using one of the asymmetric cryptography algorithms. Like most other blockchain projects, Bitcoin uses an ECDSA. As you know, the elliptic curve is described by the following equation:

$$y^2 = x^3 + ax + b$$

Bitcoin uses the form of this equation as $y^2 = x^3 + 7$. The obvious simplification should not mislead the reader – these coefficients are entirely sufficient for generating computational complexity in terms of solving the inverse problem of restoring a private key from a public one. In general, the data for the parameters of elliptic curves are taken from the recommendations of the SECG consortium responsible for developing "Standards for Efficient Cryptography" which are also used in the Bitcoin project. The parameters are calculated in such a way as to give the system the least vulnerability to attacks on ciphers created on the basis of asymmetric cryptographic methods. At present, there is no known record of a successful attempt to break the elliptic cryptography algorithm used within the SECG-recommended parameters. Quantum computers may prove capable of solving these problems, but they will need to acquire enough qubits to do so, which will take time – perhaps even a considerable amount.

Let's get back to generating keys. First, a 256-bit private key is randomly generated, and then a public key of equal length is mathematically calculated from it. However, a public key is not entirely the same thing as a Bitcoin address. In order for it to become an address, a few procedures must be carried out. First, the public key is passed sequentially through two different hashing algorithms (SHA-256 and MD5). In the latter case, its address is shortened from 256 bits to 160. Then, one byte of the network identifier (core or test network) is added to the beginning of the shortened address and to the end are attached four bytes of the checksum address, which is also a part of the hash of the shortened address. The checksum is required for verifying in cases where the address is entered manually: in case of incorrect input, the system will issue a warning. Transactions in the blockchain are irrevocable, so the sender of the cryptocurrency does not have room for error. If the address is entered incorrectly, the sender's funds will be sent "into the void." More precisely, they will be sent to an address for which none of the potential network users will have a "skeleton key" in the form of a private key. As a result, no one will be able to claim these funds, and they will thus be irretrievably lost to the system.

The final step in the procedure for obtaining a Bitcoin address is its conversion to a more "readable" form. To do this, a block of data in hexadecimal code format (using digits 0 through 9 and letters A through F) is converted by Base58 into a string containing digits along with uppercase and lowercase letters in Roman script. This procedure is necessary to remove characters from the address that can be interpreted in two ways when typing: e.g. the lowercase letter "l" and uppercase letter "I" or the uppercase letter "O" and the digit "0." All these measures aim to provide additional protection against erroneous address entry during transactions. Upon completion of all necessary the procedures, a Bitcoin address can look, for example, as follows:

> 1A1zP1eP5QGefi2DMPTfTL5SLmv7DivfNa

Now the user has their own address in the Bitcoin network, although the network itself does not know anything about it yet, since the user generated the address on a local device. However, since they have a pair of keys and an address formed from them, the user can receive crypto funds at the address and then send them to any other address as they wish. Following the first transaction, as it spreads across the network, this address will begin to be recognized as a new member of the system. This gives rise to the question: where exactly will the transaction go? It would be logical to assume that it should be included in the block, which is currently being formed by the network. However, this is not true: the transaction is first sent to the entire network through direct connections among the various nodes. Simultaneously, upon receiving a new transaction, each of the nodes checks it for "validity." The nodes check whether the sender actually has sufficient funds for the transaction desired. It is possible to carry out such a check by calculating all of the "unspent outputs" from previous transactions to the credit of the given sender. Also, the nodes also mathematically verify whether the digital electronic signature of the sender corresponds with the specified public key. This is necessary in order to ensure that the sender has the private key to the address from which they intend to spend the money. If the transaction has successfully passed all the necessary checks, then it is filed in temporary storage called "mempool."

Mempool is like a queue of transactions waiting to be included in a block. Each node independently sets the size of the mempool that it will store. A regular queue and a mempool have different forms of prioritizing incoming transactions. Whereas a usual queue orders data for processed in terms of the time of receipt, data in a mempool is ranked in terms of the amount of commission that the senders have specified for their transactions. As already mentioned, the value of the transaction fee is set by the sender independently, based on how quickly they would like this transaction to be included in the next blocks created. Since the person who creates a block retains the entire fee for all transactions included in the block, it would be logical to assume that transactions with the highest commission will be given priority for inclusion in the block.

If we consider the fact that block size in the Bitcoin network is limited to one megabyte and the average transaction size is about 300 bytes, then one block can hold about 4000 transactions which is not so much per se. The configuration of the Bitcoin network is such that a new block is created about once every ten minutes, so the bandwidth of the entire network is about seven transactions per second. During periods of high load on the network, when the number of transactions can increase significantly, the mempool starts increasing in size, while the speed of adding transactions to the blocks decreases. Therefore, in order for the transaction to get to the new block as quickly as possible, senders start increasing the commission. In December 2017, there was a record mempool size of about 140 MB, while the number of transactions in queue for being processed exceeded 200,000. However, six months later, the tension in the Bitcoin network had decreased significantly, the mempool had returned to a handful of megabytes, and the transaction processing fee had returned to normal values.

As already noted, each of the network participants, being equal in rights with the other node participants, receives on its local device (usually a normal computer) all the information about all the blocks and transactions of the Bitcoin network. As the block base grows over time, the amount of information transferred for synchronization is constantly increasing in size. Obviously, if the node has previously received information about the created blocks, this information does not require updating because it does not change over time. However, it should continue to receive information about newly created blocks, as well as locally store mempool which constantly receives new transactions that still need to be added to the blocks.

All in all, this data has a substantial size: as of spring 2019, the volume of the Bitcoin database was about 570,000 blocks and occupied about 250 gigabytes of disk space. For those who do not want to allocate space to store such a large amount of data, it could make sense to take advantage of the "light client" status, whereby instead of downloading the entirety of information, the user only downloads the block headers without a list of the transactions. In this case, such users only need to have a few hundred megabytes of information on their devices, which is incomparably faster and more lightweight than synchronizing a full database. However, in such a scenario, this "light" node will not be able to participate in the creating new blocks. However, not all of the network members are involved in this – in the spring of 2019, there were about 10,000 full nodes in the Bitcoin network and about 640,000 unique addresses in active use.

When studying the principles of the blockchain in general and the Bitcoin network in particular, one should bear in mind the mechanics of how new blocks are created in a distributed network. It is clear that only one block can be added at a time to the end of the chain, and the block is created by only one network participant. At the same time, the rest of the network must accept the block via consensus mechanisms and synchronize its own block base with the most recently created block. However, as we have seen, the network has thousands of full nodes and each of these could potentially create its own block and offer it to the rest of the network for inclusion in the common blockchain. It inevitably follows from this fact that over a short interval of time (measured in minutes), the network may have conflicting blocks seeking inclusion in the common chain. Moreover, some of the nodes might include one block, whereas other blocks opt for a different one. From this moment, the network undergoes a splitting and desynchronization of the base of blocks; in other words, there is a problem for the entire network which needs to be resolved.

In order to solve this problem, we need to consider the process of creating a block as such. To create a block, you need to gather as many transactions from the mempool as space in the block will permit and use them to calculate the Merkle root, which along with the rest of the service information will serve to generate the block header. To ensure the continuity of the blockchain, the next step is to place the hash of the previous block header in the header of the created block, after which the new block is ready and can be sent to the network for the other nodes to include in their chains. Now let's consider the following question: what if a sufficiently large number of nodes simultaneously began to offer their blocks to the rest of the network? This would undoubtedly unleash utter chaos. Communication channels would be overloaded with information sent for synchronization, there would inevitably be a huge number of different options for the branching of chains – in general, the network would actually lose its integrity and, consequently, operability.

To avoid such a negative scenario, the number of blocks offered to the network for inclusion in the chain needs to kept extremely small. Ideally, during the average time interval between the creation of blocks (in the Bitcoin network – about ten minutes), there are no competing blocks in the network at all. Yet, how can this be achieved? The answer is simple: the process of creating blocks needs to be so complex that within the quantum of time allocated for creating a new block, the network is offered a minimum number of new blocks. In this case, a necessary precondition to their creation should be solving a complex computational problem – such as described in the concept of proof-of-work. In the Bitcoin network, the process of creating a block is called "mining," by analogy with mining, where serious efforts are required before it is possible to extract a precious resource from the mine and sell it in order to obtain material benefit . How is digital mining carried out in the Bitcoin network?

Mining in the Bitcoin network

While integrating the proof-of-work concept into his BitGold project, which many people consider to be the "precursor" of Bitcoin, Nick Szabo encountered a problem where the fixed complexity of a computational problem led to a potential vulnerability that would likely manifest itself in the future. The fact is that the network's total computing power will grow organically over time. This will happen for two reasons: firstly, the total number of nodes will grow, and secondly, according to Moore's Law, the average computing power of a single system node will also gradually increase. After some time, the complexity of the computational problem built into the project logic will thus cease to pose a problem for the network. Ultimately, network nodes will turn into "printing presses" for electronic money which will inevitably induce hyperinflation throughout the system. This will certainly strip the system nodes of their material incentives, and this will call into question their future participation in such a project.

We should bear in mind that the heart of the complex problem in the BitGold project was to search through the hashes of various pre-images. Ultimately, the aim was to find a hash which would be considered valid for the entire network – i.e. in this case, that would mean a hash that contains a certain number of zeros at the beginning of the data string. The static complexity of the computational problem proved an insurmountable obstacle for Szabo and ultimately impeded BitGold from ever coming to fruition. In his Bitcoin project, however, Satoshi Nakamoto solved this problem and quite elegantly so, as we will soon see.

In fact, there is an obvious solution to this problem: if the static complexity of the problem is impeding the economic stability of the system, it must be made dynamic. As we already know, in order to get n number of zero bits at the beginning of the hash string, we need to search through at most 2^n pre-images for hashing. Obviously, the greater the number n, the greater the exponential factor by which the complexity of the problem increases. Nakamoto proposed hashing the header of the created block, starting with the smallest complexity. In this case, it was necessary to obtain only eight zero characters at the beginning of the header hash string. Since one symbol is four bits, it was not necessary to search through more than 2^{32} variants (i.e. about 4.3 billion), before then increasing the number of network nodes trying to find valid hashes, proportionately raising the complexity and thus heightening the requirements for the number of leading zeros.

When Nakamoto launched his Bitcoin network in early January 2009, there were no other participants apart from the system creator. This means that Nakamoto himself was the one who "mined" the first blocks. As other nodes began to appear in the Bitcoin network, the complexity of the network gradually began to increase. The logic of managing the complexity was as follows: the complexity of the network must be such that regardless of the number of nodes looking for blocks or their computing power, it would take no more or less time than an average of ten minutes to find a new block. The difficulty was recalculated every 2016 blocks – i.e. about once every two weeks. The total time actually spent finding all of the blocks was divided by 2016 (i.e. the number of blocks), and the result was compared with the ten-minute standard. If the blocks were on average faster, the complexity stepped up a notch, i.e. the requirements were raised for the number of zeros in the hash of the block header. If the average time was slower, then the requirements decreased.

Now, it's time for a slight digression to understand how hashes are sorted through in the mining process. Since the block header is hashed, this means that the information hashed is relatively static. In turn, this suggests that if the pre-image remains the same, we will always receive the same hash. This, however, conflicts with our goal of finding a "golden" hash that has a large number of leading zeros. For now, let's take another look at the block header structure to see if there is any dynamic value that will change so fast that the miner can hash millions, billions, or even trillions of pre-images per second?

The sequence number of the block is purely static information and not subject to change. The block version number is also a fixed value. Now, let's turn to the block creation time which is expressed in the number of seconds that have transpired since January 1, 1970. One could logically presume that it will not change more than once per second which for our purposes is an extremely low level of dynamics. In addition, the number of transactions in the block and the Merkle root value calculated from them are also relatively constant. However, there are cases when during the search for a valid hash, the miner gets access to new transactions offering a higher commission than those that they have already added to the block, at which point it would make sense to start over assembling the block. However, this procedure is somewhat static and does not adequately resolve the problems with the necessary variety of hashes.

It turns out that since the highly dynamic information in the block header is naturally absent, it is necessary to introduce an artificial element into the mining procedure to solve the problem. It will not carry any useful load, except to play the role of an additional component of the block header, as a pre-image for hashing. Such an element actually exists in the header of each block, and it is called the "nonce." During the search for the hash, the miner will be extremely fast in cycling through values of this nonce, thus making it possible to obtain an enormous number of different hashes which could potentially include the coveted "golden" hash with the required number of zeros.

In fact, the mining procedure boils down to finding a suitable value of this very nonce. When the correct nonce is added to the block header, it will allow the miner to calculate a valid hash, thus conferring on the miner the right to create a new block which will be unconditionally accepted by the entire network. However, the procedure for finding the required nonce value is far from trivial. The Bitcoin network uses the SHA-256 hashing algorithm, which involves two cycles of 64 hashing iterations each. As of spring 2019, the complexity of the Bitcoin network requires there to be 18 leading zeros to find a valid hash corresponding to 72 zero bit values. In total, this requires about 2^{72} or about $5*10^{21}$ hash iterations. Is that a lot or a little? For the sake of comparison, let's take the number of grains of sand on all the beaches of our planet. Scientists estimate the number of grains of sand to be approximately 10^{18}. This means that the complexity of finding a valid hash which satisfies all the applicable requirements could be likened to sorting through all the grains of sand on about 5000 Earth-like planets. Here is an example of such a valid hash, with a complexity requirement of 18 leading zeros:

000000000000000000001621af297d27d54b501f6a3d329399c29cf316932973ef

As already mentioned, Satoshi Nakamoto found the first blocks of the Bitcoin network on his own and used an ordinary computer for this. Similarly, the other network participants who began to gradually appear also mined their own blocks. At that very initial level of complexity, a conventional computer processor could reliably mine a block in an average of ten minutes. However, as the number of participants in the network grew, automatic recalibration resulted in the complexity beginning to increase, until at some point the computational task became "unaffordable" for a conventional computer processor to perform. Nevertheless, miners quickly found a workaround: they stopped using the CPU for the search, opting instead for the processor on their graphics cards. The specifics of its computing architecture enable the GPU to calculate hashes much faster than the CPU. With time, however, the complexity increased to such an extent that the GPU could no longer cope with the task of mining blocks. Mind you, no time was wasted in finding a solution: in June 2012, the company Butterfly Labs began supplying special computer appliances called application-specific integrated circuit (ASIC). In fact, it was a small specialized computer, fully optimized for only one task – to search through hashes generated by the SHA-256 algorithm and to do so with extreme speed. An era began of initially private and then industrial Bitcoin mining which relied on the most cutting-edge hardware produced by various companies engaged in active competition with one another.

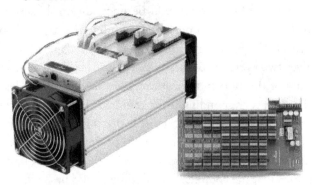

To better grasp the drastic increase in the network's complexity in the first ten years of its existence, let's have a look at notion of how quickly hashes can be searched through – i.e. the "hash rate." A distinction is made between the hash rate of a single device, and the total hash rate of the entire network. Obviously, the higher the total hash rate of the Bitcoin network, the greater the difficulty of finding a hash valid for creating a block. Otherwise, miners would find blocks too quickly, which would be a contradiction of the very logic inherent to the blockchain system. Here you can see how the hash rate changed over ten years of the Bitcoin network (as illustrated by a logarithmic graph):

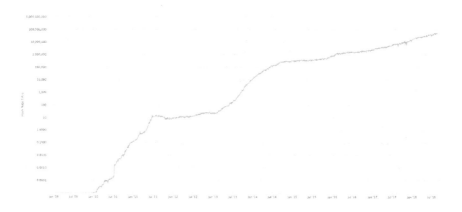

The first ASIC device operated with a hash rate of 4.5 GH/s. To put this in clearer terms, if such a device had been used at the minimum computational complexity from the very beginning of the Bitcoin network, it could have found a valid hash in about one second. This speed was 600 times higher than that at which Satoshi Nakamoto himself calculated the first blocks using the processor of his computer. A sample ASIC device from spring 2019 supplied by Bitmain can cycle through hashes with a speed of 53 TH/s, which outperforms by a factor of 10,000 the first devices introduced nearly seven years earlier. That said, the total hash rate of the Bitcoin network has attained truly astronomical peak performance figures – about 60 exahashes per second, which amounts to network-wide performance of iterating through $6*10^{19}$ hashes per second. Nevertheless, the complexity of finding a valid hash is such that even with the vast aggregate computing power of the entire network, it still takes an average time of ten minutes to mine one block. What does that mean?

This means that almost no single individual can independently mine a single block in the Bitcoin network, even if they possess a farm of hundreds or even thousands of high-speed ASIC devices – barring, of course, some phenomenal degree of luck which would certainly not be repeatable in the long run. Therefore, miners combine their forces via huge computing pools and thus distribute both the complexity of the task and the reward for its solution proportionally among the pool participants in accordance with the computing power contributed. The first such pool opened on September 18, 2010, before the advent of ASIC devices when mining was mainly carried out with processors and graphics cards. With time, more of these pools started popping up, and then they began to consolidate into larger associations of miners from around the world.

The issue of mining farms combined into computing pools provides a smooth segue to the main problem of mining based on proof-of-work consensus: the exceptionally large amount of electricity consumed to operate the mining equipment. The modern, high-speed ASIC BitmainS17 Pro consumes 2250 watts, which is a significant amount, especially when you consider that the entire mining farm is comprised of such devices. In addition, while mining, these devices heat up significantly such that they need to be constantly cooled down, which also consumes electricity. When putting together a mining farm, the entrepreneur has the primary costs of purchase and delivery of the mining equipment as well as the rent and equipment costs for the room where the farm will actually operate.

Nonetheless, the heftiest expenditure in this farming operation will be paying for the electricity consumption necessary for mining. This cost alone is the most critical factor in calculating the profitability of mining various cryptocurrencies – primarily Bitcoin. The total annual amount of electricity consumed by the entire Bitcoin network is on par with that consumed by one of the top 30 countries in terms of electricity usage. We are talking about the value of 30–35 terawatt-hours per year, which is approximately equivalent to 0.5–0.6% of total electricity consumption worldwide. Analysts have predicted that if the current rate of growth in electricity consumption by the Bitcoin network remains steady, then in three to four years Bitcoin miners will begin to consume all the electricity produced in the world. Obviously, such a scenario cannot be considered tenable: state regulators simply will not permit it.

For this reason, the future outlook of mining based on the proof-of-work consensus seems somewhat hazy. It is very likely that many national governments will begin to limit miners in their consumption of electricity – e.g. by establishing regulatory quotas which must be purchased at special auctions. It is also possible that in some countries where the shortage of electricity is particularly acute, mining will be completely prohibited by law. The most problematic aspect of this entire issue is that all the electricity is being consumed to solve a mathematical problem, which loses its value every ten minutes. In other words, once a new block is created, the solution of the problem starts over from scratch. Obviously, this is an extremely inefficient use of such a valuable resource as electricity – it is actually wasted without providing any significant benefit to human civilization (except for the owners and employees of energy companies).

This large amount of computing power could be dedicated to solving truly urgent problems, such as the calculations associated with the search for new medicines or other scientific problems that require serious calculations. Perhaps, cryptocurrency mining in the future will evolve in a manner more efficient for the global community, when the computational work in finding blocks will be aimed at solving useful scientific problems. Although examples of such projects already exist, they have not yet gained popularity. Otherwise, when creating blocks, the crypto community will find itself obliged to adopt forms of achieving consensus which are much less energy-intensive than proof-of-work. And such protocols are also actively being developed and tested, so that later they can assume a leading position in the technological process of creating new blocks.

Returning to the issue of mining blocks in the Bitcoin network, we begin to view this as a rather expensive procedure for those who invest their material assets in it. As such, there should be direct monetary incentive to ensure that there will always be individuals interested in performing this work. As mentioned earlier, once miners have created a block, they retain for themselves the entire commission from the transactions which they added to the block. Yet, the combined value of these fees does not quite justify the costs incurred by those responsible for keeping up the costly mining infrastructure. Moreover, there is another important issue to which we have not yet given due consideration: in order to start carrying out monetary transactions in the Bitcoin network, these funds must initially appear in the network from somewhere. As such, the main reward for those who are fortunate enough to successfully implement the creation of the block is called the block reward. We are talking about an amount expressed in digital bitcoins which the miner receives when each new block is created. Now, we have laid the groundwork for a "cryptocurrency" and used by way of example the digital coins in the Bitcoin network. What are these coins, how do they appear in the Bitcoin network and in what quantity, and what kind of material value can they have?

Bitcoin as a cryptocurrency

What could seemingly be simpler than the process of issuing electronic money? It does not require expending resources such as those used in the process of minting metal coins or printing paper banknotes. If an electronic money system has already been created and is successfully operating, the supervisory body can directly issue new digital coins by merely entering the desired size of the emission into the system settings. However, with such centralized management of money emissions, there is no guarantee that the owners of the system will not be carried away by excessive "printing" of non-backed electronic money, since this will inevitably unleash uncontrolled hyperinflation. Also, this would simultaneously result in the money losing value as a means of payment as well as the trust of system users.

When setting up the Bitcoin system, Satoshi Nakamoto was undoubtedly aware of the fact that electronic money could easily become superfluous, so he took care in advance to ensure that his system would be resistant to such vulnerabilities. First of all, he developed a mechanism of mining in the form of a complex computational task which is solved in a decentralized and competitive manner. In order to provide miners with significant monetary incentive, the decision was made that each newly created block would also bring a small monetary emission. As the value of the digital coin rises, this emission should decrease over time. This process will continue until the total number of coins issued by the system reaches the final value laid down in the system design.

Initially, Nakamoto established that at the time of launching the system, the reward in exchange for creating a block would be 50 bitcoins. Then, every four years, this number would be halved until the total number of bitcoins in the system equaled 21 million coins. According to mathematical projections, the last bitcoin in the system will be created around 2140, while by 2036 more than 99% of all coins will have been received. Once all the coins have been issued and the reward for creating a block falls to zero, miners will have to settle for the transaction fee, which they will retain for themselves when creating new blocks. It is presumed that by that time, the cost of one bitcoin will have risen to such an extent that miners will remain incentivized even without a block reward since the transaction fee which they collect will more than compensate for all their mining-related costs.

By mid-2018, the block reward had already been cut twice from the original Nakamoto value – first in 2012 to 25 bitcoins and then in 2016 to 12.5. The next decrease in remuneration is expected in May 2020, when it will fall to 6.25 bitcoins. That said, the total transaction fee could reach prices of one bitcoin or even more. However, this would only be the case in times of heightened network load due to the large number of transactions, thus inducing a spike in the fee for them to be added to the block. Typically, however, when the network load becomes more readily manageable, the aggregate fee of all transactions in the blocks is much smaller.

By capping the maximum possible volume of bitcoins following the last emission at 21 million coins, Nakamoto's primary objective was to introduce protection against inflation. The project creator hoped that the value of bitcoin in the future would show stable growth and could ultimately attain serious levels of value. Therefore, it has been determined that each bitcoin can be divided into one hundred million parts, or in other words, have eight decimal places. The smallest unit of 0.00000001 bitcoin later became known as a "satoshi" in honor of the creator of the Bitcoin system. It isn't difficult to see that if the emission limit is strictly limited, then instead of inflation, the system will instead be faced with deflation, whereby all the goods and services denominated in bitcoins will eventually experience a depreciation in value. Yet, even if someday the cost of a single satoshi amounts to one cent on the US dollar, the total value of all bitcoins will equate to approximately USD 21 trillion which would certainly suffice for making this cryptocurrency a mass payment system on the global scale.

Compared to traditional forms of money, bitcoins are heavily protected from unauthorized reproduction by cryptographic mathematical algorithms. However, even the Bitcoin system has one vulnerability, albeit one which is even theoretically quite difficult to exploit. This vulnerability is called a "51% attack" and refers to a scenario where there appears in the network a node (or a group of nodes) with exceptional processing power comprising more than 50% of the total network hash rate. In other words, these nodes begin to mine new blocks faster than the rest of the network. In the Bitcoin network, there is a rule that if the system forms branches within the blockchain, the network takes the longer branch for the legitimate one. Thus, the shorter branch with all the blocks included in it is simply not accepted by the network and therewith discarded. This also implies automatic exclusion of all transactions that have been placed in the blocks of a branch which has not been accepted by the network.

In such a scenario, the mere fact of adding a transaction to one of the blocks is clearly not sufficient. According to the rules, a certain amount of time is required to ensure that a transaction does not fall into a branch of blocks that could be discarded in favor of a longer, alternative chain. It is generally assumed that none of the parallel branches can be longer than six blocks; in other words, the probability of such a situation is extremely small. It thus follows that six confirmations for any transaction in the Bitcoin network is enough for it to be considered unequivocally completed. To put it another way, if five more blocks were added to the chain in a row following a block containing a transaction, then this amounts to the same six confirmations necessary for the transaction to be recognized as completed (one block equals one confirmation). In other words, it takes about six ten-minute segments to fully confirm a transaction. Coming back to the "51% attack problem," imagine that some node has assumed computational dominance in the network and that their blocks have begun to be placed in the chain acknowledged as the true one. Why is this bad for the network as a whole?

First, the dominance of a single node or a group of them united by a common goal can lead to scenarios where this consortium of attackers can assume entire control over the mining of blocks and, thus, all of the network's new transactions. In addition to the fact that this would constitute a de facto monopoly over the mining proceeds, they could be selective in their choice of transactions to be added to blocks. Above all, this would include transactions that allow coins to be reused – i.e. "double spending." The only thing outside of their power would be interfering with the data of previously created blocks – even 51% of the computational power would not be enough. This issue is that this would require recalculating all the block hashes, starting with the one changed and all the way through to the last one in the chain taking into account the modifications made. As a result, you will need to find new nonces for all the reassembled blocks and offer the network a new chain – and a fairly long one at that. At the same time, the rest of the network will continue to count off and form blocks, starting with the last one to be accepted by the entire network (i.e. a much later block than the last one in the attackers' calculations). As regards the issue of double spending, it can indeed become a serious problem. By the way, it was this very issue that had stood in the way of creating decentralized money in the "pre-blockchain" era. To understand why a 51% attack would enable double spending, consider the following example.

Suppose that you have a node in your network that has more processing power than all the other nodes combined. This node selects one of the blocks as a "reference point" and begins to mine new blocks from it, without showing them for some time to the rest of the network. At the same time, the user will spend the crypto funds which they have remaining in the main chain while they wait to receive confirmation from the network for the blocks which they have created. As such, at least five more blocks will appear in the main chain after the one containing the spending transactions of the malicious node. Then the node will reveal to the entire network the alternative chain which it created in parallel, and it will be longer because the collective processing power of this node exceeded that of all the others. As a result, the network will be forced to recognize this branch as the valid one. Any old blocks previously designed and validated by the whole network will have to be discarded, which means attributing to them the status of so-called "orphaned blocks" no longer having connection to the main chain. It logically follows that all of the spending transactions of the malicious node will also be thus discarded, as if they had never existed at all.

It should come as no surprise that the alternative blocks proposed to the network by the rogue node will not contain any record of expenditure transactions belonging to it. Thus, despite the fact that in a "previous reality," the attacker spent theirs and in exchange for said funds received some goods, services, or even another cryptocurrency, after some time they can simply credit their assets back to themselves and the network will be obliged to accept this. This would seem to be a disastrous issue for any blockchain system that creates proof-of-work blocks. However, in practice, implementing such a scenario is extremely difficult –both organizationally and monetarily – and in some cases it may not even make practical sense. Let's try to explain why.

For starters, putting together such an attack is easy only in theory. Imagine how much computing power would be needed to take over more than half of the hash rate of any network – especially the Bitcoin network, where the total hash rate is astronomically large. To assess the effectiveness of such attacks for attackers, one needs to think in terms of the "cost of attack." Generally speaking, engaging high-level computational resources is an exceptionally expensive endeavor. If we are talking about the level of computational capacity required to attack a network as powerful as Bitcoin, then at least a few nearly unsolvable problems emerge.

Firstly, there is the physical impossibility of using the required number of computers or ASIC devices for such an operation, as it is simply unrealistic to consolidate such a volume of devices under unified management. Presuming even that the government of a country like the United States wanted to carry out such an attack in order to gain control of the Bitcoin network, the likelihood that a state structure of such stature could manage something similar would be virtually non-existent. Secondly, one must take into account the cost of engaging this amount of computational resources. Quite probably, the costs incurred would outweigh the theoretical economic gain to be obtained from a successful attack.

And last but not least, after a successful attack on a cryptocurrency, there would ensue an overall loss of confidence in the currency itself. Undoubtedly, the market price for it would fall to almost zero, while ruining all the system participants, including the attacker. Obviously, the networks with the greatest vulnerability to such attacks are the "young" ones with a relatively low hash rate and, therefore, a lower cost of attack. In such cases, the attack does not even intend to carry out double spending, but rather to damage the networks in order to destroy them or at least to shut down their operation for some time. After all, the node that has gained control of the network decides which transactions will be included in the blocks and which will not. Plus, it can create, for example, only empty blocks without transactions, thus paralyzing any cryptocurrency transfers within the attacked network.

In the history of the Bitcoin network, there was a case on June 13, 2014 when for a few hours the Ghash mining pool took over 51% of the entire network's computing power. This was caused naturally by a significant increase in the number of participants in the pool. However, immediately after the hash rate was exceeded, many members of the pool stopped their mining processes, and the pool itself stopped registering and connecting new users. This was done intentionally in order to prevent possible destructive consequences for the network as a whole. With time, the total hash rate of the Bitcoin network had grown so significantly that such situations could no longer arise for any of these pools.

In any case, as already noted, the main negative result of gaining computational control over the network would be a catastrophic erosion of the trust of participants in the system as a whole. In such an event, one could almost certainly expect a serious drop in the worth of the affiliated cryptocurrency as valued in classical fiat currency. Fiat currency refers to the typical world currencies issued by national governments or groups of governments, such as the European Union. Fiat money is what we all use on a daily basis, and this term will repeatedly be used throughout this book to designate the opposite of cryptocurrency as a means of payment.

Since the direct use of cryptocurrencies for purchasing real goods or services is still insufficiently developed, most miners still go through the daily necessity of exchanging their hard-earned cryptocurrency for fiat currency. For this reason, the exchange rate of cryptocurrency for fiat currency is exceptionally important for all network participants (and first of all active miners themselves). While it is clear that the fiat equivalent of cryptocurrency reflects its value, how then can this value be determined? What primarily affects the exchange rates of cryptocurrencies in general and bitcoin in particular?

Bitcoin as an asset

Nine days after the launch of the Bitcoin network – January 12, 2009 – Satoshi Nakamoto carried out the very first transaction on the network. As a test, he sent a dozen bitcoins to another member of the network who joined almost immediately after Nakamoto himself. It turned out to be the American programmer and cryptoenthusiast Hal Finney who in 2004 wrote the first proof-of-work algorithm for the PGP protocol software that provides public-key encryption functionality. The transaction was included in block number 170 and became the first historical blockchain transaction conducted between two members of the network. Is it reasonable to assume that for testing purposes Satoshi Nakamoto parted ways with digital coins whose total value in under ten years would be worth tens and even hundreds of thousands of dollars? At the time of the first transaction, bitcoin had no monetary value. How did it happen that soon thereafter serious amounts of fiat money started being spent on cryptocurrency exchanges?

In order to answer this question, it would make sense to take a look at what comprises the value of a bitcoin. The history of ordinary money is well known: at first there were only coins made of precious metals, like gold and silver. In this case, they had an inherent value. Then human civilization switched to paper banknotes which were initially backed by the gold reserves of state banks and then by the gross domestic product after the abolition of the gold standard. If nothing else, this is how national governments explain it. In reality, the real situation is much more complicated as the national economy of each state is constantly faced with such phenomena as inflation, unemployment, foreign debt, and other macroeconomic factors. Each of them has its impact on the value of the national currency, including the fluctuation of its exchange rate in relation to the currencies of other countries.

All national currencies, being formally secured property of the respective states, are protected from fraud, insofar as this is technologically possible. To this end, special methods are employed for making banknote paper, a special printing ink is used, and additional security elements are applied to banknotes, such as watermarks, serial numbering, and holographic images. All this, of course, does not give an absolute guarantee against money potentially being counterfeited; however, in the vast majority of cases, people do not have problems with trust in paper banknotes. Popular trust in fiat money derives from the following factors:

- governmental recognition of the paper banknotes as legal tender;
- the fact that the national currency is backed by the gross domestic product, as well as the national gold and foreign exchange reserves;
- restriction of monetary emissions with the aim of curbing potential inflation;
- physical protection of banknotes against counterfeiting;
- trust from other people willing to accept banknotes for payment;
- the relatively stable exchange rate of the national currency in relation to the currencies of other states.

Generally speaking, if even one of the above-mentioned factors were no longer true, the credibility of the national currency would be significantly undermined such that it could lose its suitability for day-to-day use. Not so long ago, Zimbabwe experienced something similar when exceptional hyperinflation forced the citizens to completely switch to making payments in US dollars. Venezuela is also undergoing something similar with its national currency – the bolivar – which was subject to large-scale depreciation. In fact, a situation arose where basic food purchases could only be made with literal mounds of banknotes that were no longer worth the paper on which they were printed.

Now, let's switch back to bitcoin and check out the same trust factors that were listed in relation to fiat money. Since bitcoin is a decentralized form of digital money that does not have a single emission center controlled by any sovereign state, there is no talk yet of its recognition as an official means of payment. More precisely, this could happen at some point in the future, but each individual state will have to take its own stance on this issue. And it may well be that opinions are split: some countries will opt to recognize bitcoin and other cryptocurrencies as a means of payment, while others will not.

Now, as concerns restricting monetary emissions, we have seen that the emission of bitcoin is finite in its volume and is limited to 21 million coins. In this way, the bitcoin project entirely sidesteps the issue of potential inflation, and, importantly, the guarantee of protection does not rest on some promise from some government to control inflationary processes, but rather on strict compliance with the project's mathematical logic. Protection against counterfeiting operates on the same principle: the emission of bitcoins is a purely mathematical process based on complex cryptographic problems being solved in a decentralized manner. Therefore, unlike with conventional banknotes, Bitcoin offers a mathematically proven guarantee that "extra" digital coins will not appear in the system.

One of the main critiques of bitcoin is that it lacks asset backing. This issue merits a slightly more in-depth discussion. In the description of the proof-of-work concept in one of the previous chapters, we analyzed as an example what can underpin the value of gold. Among other arguments, it was demonstrated how many steps precede the moment when gold finally becomes available for purchase – i.e. specialists must be engaged for geological exploration, mining, casting, freight transport, industrial production of finished goods, and finally their sale to the final consumer. Clearly, under normal market circumstances, the value of a gold product – whether an ingot, a coin, or a piece of jewelry – cannot be less than the sum total of labor and material resources spent on its production. We should also include the built-in income at each stage of the "value chain," and as a result we will get a logically justified cost for the final product – i.e. the minimum price required for there to be any commercial sense.

Now, let's extend this analogy to the processes of mining cryptocurrencies and bitcoin, in particular. In this instance, we will also see a chain of added value which is quite similar to the manufacturing process for any other product (including gold). In order to mine, you must purchase computers or specialized mining equipment, rent and equip a facility for the crypto farm, pay for the electricity necessary to operate the ASIC mining devices, pay the wages of IT specialists responsible for farm maintenance, make tax payments, and this list of costs for the mining entrepreneur is not exhaustive. By extension, this means that for each bitcoin mined, there is a set sum of expenses which sets a lower value threshold of sorts for the value of the final product: a cryptocurrency coin. When Satoshi Nakamoto mined his first bitcoins, due to the minimal complexity of the network, his costs were close to zero, just like the value of a bitcoin at that time. However, years later, the mining process has become a very costly event.

Many believe that bitcoin – like any other cryptocurrency mined on the basis of a proof-of-work consensus – is backed only by the electricity spent to produce it. Of course, that is one way of putting it, but as we have seen, bitcoin mining requires much more than electricity alone, even if it admittedly accounts for the largest share of the expenses. Due to this kind of variable cost, miners make a substantial effort to avoid, in their jargon, "falling lower than the outlet." In other words, the fiat price of a bitcoin should not be less than the cost of electricity consumed to obtain it. Given that the market value of electricity continually rises with the passing of time – in the same way that the amount of energy expenditure required to extract one coin grows – during periods of particularly significant negative fluctuations in the bitcoin exchange rate on the exchanges, mining can bring losses.

Oddly enough, the talented creator of the Bitcoin project foresaw such a scenario – after all, the complexity of coin mining is automatically controlled by the network in both directions. And if it becomes unprofitable for miners to maintain their farms at some level of complexity, they can abandon this activity and turn off their equipment, temporarily or indefinitely. At this point, the total hash rate of the network will begin to drop as will its proportionate complexity, thus reducing the amount of electricity needed to produce a single cryptocoin. That said, even with a considerable dip from the peak prices in the bitcoin exchange rate, the total computing power of the network is still actively increasing.

In 2018 alone, the hash rate in the Bitcoin network tripled, despite the fact that over the course of the year, the price of bitcoin tumbled to nearly one quarter of its previous value. Admittedly, the inexhaustible optimism of miners and their faith in the recovery and further growth of the value of bitcoin prove stronger than a realistic analysis of the market situation. Thus, there is every reason to believe that the vast majority of miners tend to consider periods of price correction to be merely passing phenomena. By the same token, upward price trends are widely considered to be more long lasting.

Ultimately, one of the factors with the greatest impact on the amount of trust that a given individual places in a cryptocurrency is their perception of how widespread of trust it receives from other market participants. It is precisely this aggregate trust at the level of society which also contributes substantially to the value of any financial asset, including cryptocurrencies. When paper money began to appear in Europe in the 18th century, popular acceptance of it remained quite feeble. For thousands of years, all trade relations had been based on the circulation of coins made of precious metals – primarily gold. Admittedly, the indigenous peoples of America in the era prior to Columbus's arrival were somewhat aloof from these processes. They used gold for seemingly everything but money – at least until the conquistadors "drew" them into the global financial system. As for paper banknotes, popular trust was a work of evolution that unfolded over the course of centuries. Moreover, this was all despite the fact that up until just before the abolition of the gold standard in the 1970s, state banks continued to guarantee the exchange of banknotes for gold from their reserves.

Thus, one finds oneself led to the inexorable conclusion that trust in various forms of means of payment is a question of everyday habits and routines, which can take hundreds or even thousands of years for people to develop. Plus, what it ultimately amounts to is the centuries-old reputation of the materials used for making the money, as well as that of the issuers themselves who release the money into circulation. In the eyes of many people, the fact that cryptocurrencies are an electronic (more at, physically intangible) form of money makes them novel and, thus, somewhat unusual. Nonetheless, as we saw earlier, cryptocurrencies do indeed offer a series of serious advantages over fiat money. Moreover, the role of the issuer in this case is assumed by mathematical algorithms, whose reputation is strictly scientific and therefore unobjectionable.

It would thus seem difficult to presume that people on a large scale could grow comfortable with and accustomed to using a fundamentally new form of money over the mere ten years that the blockchain technology has existed. However, there is every reason to believe that this payment system will become commonplace at a global scale much faster than its historical predecessors – particularly if you consider how the market rate of the first cryptocurrency performed in its first years of existence. At some point, the crypto community began to consider bitcoin not only as a utilitarian means of fast, anonymous, and inexpensive payment, but also as a form of financial investment. Many investors had good reason to believe that such investments could bring them a significant income in a relatively short period of time. To what extent have their expectations been justified?

Bitcoin as an investment

In the early stages of the Bitcoin network, not many people engaged in mining cryptocurrencies at low levels of complexity took it very seriously. They saw it more as a game rather than as part of a new type of financial system. Consequently, when the miners received their first bitcoins, they acted accordingly: performing test transfers for one another, giving them away as gifts, discarding them for lack of utility, or simply losing track of them along with the secret keys to their digital wallets. Nevertheless, on October 5, 2009, bitcoin received its first ever market monetary valuation based on actual transactions. One US dollar could fetch 1309 bitcoins – i.e. one bitcoin was equal to about 0.08 US cents.

However, the rate quickly took a sharp turn upwards. In this regard, I would like to mention one story that happened in late 2009 in Norway, where a local student named Christopher Koch was writing a thesis on cryptography. He decided to devote one of the sections of his thesis to a relatively recent phenomenon in the field of cryptography known as the Bitcoin project. During his research, he made a test purchase of 5000 bitcoins for an amount approximately equivalent to USD 27. Per coin, this worked out to a little more than one half of a cent. After writing and successfully defending his thesis, Koch blissfully forgot about the bitcoins that he had purchased. However, about four years later, he found ample reason to revisit this purchase, when this cryptocurrency began the object of intense popularity and global renown. Upon realizing that he was the owner of a significant number of digital coins, he hastily started looking for his long-abandoned virtual assets. Only with great difficulty did he manage to find the password for his bitcoin wallet, but the effort proved well worth it. It turned out that in the matter of a few years, his half-forgotten casual investment of USD 27 had turned into a precious treasure worth about USD 1 million. In other words, during this time, the cost of one bitcoin skyrocketed to a value hundreds of times larger. Koch's graduate work effectively made him a wealthy man – and most quickly so. After spending a fair share of his wealth which seemingly appeared out of thin air on real estate, Koch decided to save a portion of the cryptocoins in his wallet in the hope that bitcoin would post further growth; indeed, its pace did not slacken over the next few years.

Yet not all stories had such happy endings. A far more famous episode in the history of Bitcoin was the first-ever purchase of physical goods with a cryptocurrency. It happened at the end of May 2010, when the American programmer Laszlo Hanyecz posted on the Bitcoin forum cry that he would pay 10,000 bitcoins to anyone who could deliver two pizzas (worth about USD 25) to the city of Jacksonville, Florida. It took four days to find a counterparty to the transaction, after which the pizzas were delivered to the designated address and the corresponding amount of bitcoins was transferred as payment. This transpired on May 22, and that spring day has now become the first and only memorable day for the entire blockchain industry and was dubbed BitcoinPizzaDay. On this day, cryptoenthusiasts around the world eat pizza and in not very flattering terms discuss the visionary talents of the hapless miner who paid the equivalent of tens of millions of dollars for two pizzas. Seven years later, that was the approximate value of ten thousand bitcoins. However, it would not be entirely accurate to assert that bitcoin's value only rose over the first ten years of its existence. Like any other financial instrument, the price of bitcoin was subject to various fluctuations and corrections due to a variety of factors – both technical and fundamental.

About a year after the launch of the Bitcoin project, the first trading platform for exchanging bitcoins for fiat currency appeared. More precisely, the BitcoinMarket exchange began its work on February 6, 2010. However, in the early period of organized bitcoin trading, it was another exchange platform that acquired the greatest fame: Mt. Gox. It opened on July 17, 2010 and quickly gained popularity among bitcoin traders, becoming the "number one exchange" for conducting transactions with cryptocurrency. Strictly speaking, the Mt. Gox project site was launched back in 2006 to organize the electronic trading of game cards of the popular table game "Magic: The Gathering." In fact, the exchange derived its name from the abbreviation of the game's name. In the spring of 2011, developer Jed McCaleb, the creator of the exchange, sold the project to French programmer Mark Karpelès who at the time was living in Japan.

This was around the time of the first "boom" of cryptocurrency trading, and the price of bitcoin began to grow. However, in June of the same year, the exchange was attacked by hackers. As a result, tens of thousands of bitcoins were stolen from exchange accounts; at the time, the value of a single bitcoin was estimated at about USD 32. Despite the fact that the "hole" in the security of the system was quickly eliminated, investment confidence in bitcoin was seriously undermined. The exchange owner and their staff exerted an enormous effort to stem the panic among traders. After that, the bitcoin exchange rate slowly resumed its growth, gradually "winning back" the losses sustained. Fully taking into account the experience of the attack conducted, Karpelès undertook serious efforts to improve the security of the exchange. Among other measures, two-factor authentication was introduced based on one-time password generators used by traders when logging into the exchange.

The following three years saw a peak of prosperity and affluence for Mt. Gox, although this period also had its own difficulties. At some point, the activities of the trading platform drew the attention of US financial regulators. As a result, the American division of the exchange experienced a blocking of accounts which housed about USD 4.5 million. The funds were ultimately returned, but it did not solve all the problems with the American banking system as a whole. Representatives of the American financial industry were very skeptical about the activities of the exchange, suspecting it of complicity in mass money laundering through cryptocurrency trading.

Nevertheless, the bitcoin exchange rate continued its climb, and by November 2013 it had surpassed the threshold of USD 1200 per bitcoin. At that time, nearly half of all transactions on the Bitcoin network, took place on the Mt. Gox exchange. However, at the same time, the operation of the exchange began to show signs of failure as seen in the delays in withdrawals of customer funds from Mt. Gox accounts – both cryptocurrencies and fiat currencies. Traders began to show discontent, and many of them opted for competitor stock exchanges. Persistent rumors about internal problems in Mt. Gox began to circulate in the blockchain environment until the intrigue finally reached its tragic conclusion in February 2014. Since the beginning of February, the exchange had not been conducting any operations to withdraw funds from accounts. On February 23, Karpelès issued a brief message about the complete collapse of the stock exchange, at which point the project site disappeared from the internet.

As one might be expected, panic broke out among the exchange's clients. On some blockchain forums, information appeared in the form of a leaked internal document from the exchange which claimed that hackers had stolen 744,000 bitcoins from exchange accounts. A few days later, on February 28, the exchange management filed for bankruptcy. This did not curb the most negative impact on the bitcoin exchange rate which sank as low as 550 USD. Officially, a loss of 650,000 bitcoins was acknowledged; yet, it proved impossible to find out whether a hacker attack really took place or the collapse was instigated by the owner themselves. There were suspicions that Karpelès transferred a substantial amount of bitcoins belonging to stock traders to a secret address in the hope of subsequently using them for personal purposes. Despite the willingness that he demonstrated in cooperating with the investigation, in spring 2019 Karpelès was sentenced to two and a half years in prison. During the investigation and legal proceedings, the bankrupt project managers managed to return to the exchange clients a portion of the funds which they managed to uncover and consolidate for subsequent payments. After the collapse of Mt.Gox, it took bitcoin about three years to regain the lofty price positions of prior years. In addition, the number of cryptocurrency exchanges had increased significantly over the same period. At present, there are hundreds of trading platforms on the internet, actively offering services for exchanging various digital coins for one another and for fiat forms of payment.

By the end of 2017, around the blockchain industry there was a situation that the crypto community began to refer to as *hype*. This period was marked by a particularly sharp growth of almost all cryptocurrencies and, most notably, bitcoin. In the run-up to Christmas, the exchange rate of the main cryptocurrency continued setting price records, before ultimately exceeding USD 20,000. By this point, the only ones not to have heard of Bitcoin were the lazy and those far removed from the world of information and financial technologies. However, since January 2018, Bitcoin has undergone a serious price correction, hemorrhaging about 75% of its value during the year. As a result, many investors who found themselves sufficiently emboldened to purchase bitcoin at the price peak suffered serious financial losses. However, those who made investments in the first half of 2017 or earlier remain comfortably in the black, as the price hike in the second half of the year was formidable. Even in freefall conditions, both indirect and direct stakeholders – investors and stakeholders – remain unshaken in their loyalty to the future of bitcoin. This category of entrepreneurs continues to ensure exceptionally high rate of growth in the Bitcoin network's hash rate – despite the fact that mining is at present essentially unprofitable and sometimes even entails sustaining losses. It's worth calling attention to the factors that affect the efficiency of operations for mining bitcoin and similar cryptocurrencies which are mined on the basis of the proof-of-work principle.

We have already called attention to the fact that entrepreneurs wishing to engage in this activity have to invest significant funds to purchase mining equipment and fit out the premises where it will be installed. In addition, miners bear the costs associated with the heightened electricity consumption, labor wages for the system engineers, deduction of tax payments, and so on. It thus logically follows that many places in the world are not suitable for effective cryptocurrency mining. Locations must be chosen where the financial costs listed above can be minimized, to the extent possible for the entrepreneur. It turns out that there are not so many places in the world where the effectiveness of mining justifies the "mining farmer's" costs – i.e. does not outweigh profit from selling the mined cryptocurrencies, especially in the conditions of a significant correction in their market value.

At the moment, the cryptomining industry has a situation where about 80% of the mining capacity has crystallized in the global industrial blacksmith's shop: in China. This is where the conditions have naturally developed which are most conducive to this type of activity; however, the Chinese government has admittedly adopted a somewhat unfriendly and frankly skeptical stance on cryptocurrencies in general. Nevertheless, the primary equipment for mining is made in China, so local miners can sidestep the expensive for international deliveries halfway around the globe as well as the additional costs for customs payments. Power plants in the mountainous regions of the country provide reasonable prices for electricity, and the relatively cold climate in these regions provides a fairly budget-friendly solution to the problem of equipment overheating. If a technological solution is chosen in favor of water cooling, then, as a rule, cold mountain rivers flow in the same vicinity to the great convenience of the miners. In the peripheral areas of China, labor wages remain relatively low, which is another important factor in favor of choosing this country for investment in cryptocurrency mining activities.

It is believed that there are four mining pools responsible for the vast majority of the computing power of the Bitcoin network, and they are all located in China. Such a high concentration of aggregate hash rate in a single political jurisdiction and under the control of only four governing entities certainly cannot be a positive factor for a technology designed to be authentically decentralized. However, the crypto community views this as a temporary phenomenon and believes that mining in the Bitcoin network will evolve over time into a more distributed form. In any case, it is bitcoin that continues to boast the strongest figures in terms of popularity and demand. Plus, the total value of all the bitcoins in circulation accounts for nearly half of the entire cryptocurrency market's capitalization. The Bitcoin project was created by Satoshi Nakamoto as a decentralized digital payment system, and the bitcoins themselves were intended to become a popular means of payment, which would gradually chase the usual fiat money out of everyday circulation. Let's try to estimate to what extent the Bitcoin project managed to implement its plan in the first decade of its existence.

Bitcoin as a means of payment

Once the digital coins of the Bitcoin network received a serious monetary valuation in the financial market, individuals with significant holdings of these digital assets became genuinely wealthy people – to the great surprise of the public (and perhaps to the surprise of the owners themselves!). Many of them possess cryptocurrency capital estimated at hundreds of millions – and in some cases billions – of dollars. Of course, as the creator of the Bitcoin project, Satoshi Nakamoto was the first person to draw attention. Being the first miner in the network which he created, he managed to get a large number of coins, since the initial level of complexity of the system was very conducive to such. At one point, people were conjecturing that Nakamoto owned approximately 1 million coins; more recent studies, however, suggest that this number does not exceed 700,000. Even so, current capitalization projections place his fortune around USD 3.5 billion. Thus, the mysterious inventor found themselves ranked alongside other world billionaires in the Forbes magazine, and during the heyday of Bitcoin's price records, Nakamoto even edged close to the title of the World's 50th Wealthiest Person.

For this reason, it is impossible not to recall the high-profile Winklevoss twin brothers – Cameron and Tyler. The former Harvard students and once Olympic athletes managed to sue Facebook creator Mark Zuckerberg for about USD 65 million in compensation for the idea of the social network which Zuckerberg had allegedly stolen from them. The brothers somewhat fortuitously invested a portion of their settlement money in bitcoin, when it still cost little more than USD 100 per coin. The presumption is that they acquired more than 100,000 bitcoins, which makes them the owners of a fortune close to USD 500 million (depending, of course, on the fluctuations of the market rate of bitcoin on the exchanges). There were rumors that the enterprising brothers had printed the secret keys to their bitcoin addresses on paper which was then cut into several parts, with each piece being separately place in bank safes in different US cities. This complex operation was carried out with the intention of protecting their digital assets from possible theft by network attackers.

And finally, it is worth mentioning once again the former owner of the Mt. Gox exchange Mark Karpelès, suspected of embezzling approximately 650,000 bitcoins, which he claims were stolen by hackers. If he indeed is secretly in possession of this treasure, its current appraisal would amount to more than USD 3 billion, which is comparable to the wealth of Nakamoto. As concerns the case of the inventor of the blockchain technology, however, the legitimacy of his purchase of bitcoins cannot be called into question, since they were obtained via entirely transparent mining processes.

A number of payment systems have been built on the basis of blockchain technology, where there is a significant number of active participants capable of accumulating certain amounts of cryptocoins. This begs the legitimate question: what goods and services could be purchased with this digital money? In reality, the answer is clear: the exact same as with fiat currency. The only issue is whether sellers are willing to accept cryptocurrency as payment. In turn, the issue for them is a question of legitimizing any income from cryptocurrency as well as their convertibility to fiat money for the purpose of their statutory accounting and tax records. Clearly, each government must solve these issues within the framework of national financial legislation, and unfortunately many places exist where the conditions are not immediately favorable for conducting cryptocurrency payments. For this reason, the purchase of goods and services for cryptocurrencies has not yet come into mass circulation. However, this process is slowly but surely taking over various business areas, and there is hope that sooner or later cryptocurrencies will take their rightful place in the circulation of commodities and money.

Occasionally, various global media outlets publish advertising messages that a particular asset can be purchased with bitcoins or other cryptocurrency. As a rule, these are luxury goods like expensive villas, yachts, posh cars, or private jets. In recent years, however, information has been increasingly popping up that you can use digital money for purchasing the most ordinary items from day-to-day life. For the time being, such points of sale remain few and far between and are almost solely represented by online stores with a relatively poor product range. After all, in order for this type of payment to become mainstream, there must be an extensive infrastructure of payment systems that will provide cash flows with the necessary conversions from one form of money to another. Such systems have already undertaken active development of their activities in various regions of the world, despite the fact that only Japan is the only national entity to have recognized cryptocurrencies as an official means of payment.

In addition to payment systems, there is another element which is vital for the successful introduction of cryptocurrencies into mass circulation – an

ATM that issues fiat cash for bitcoins or other popular cryptocurrencies. Some projects are already working on creating and installing such monetary devices, and the volume of their global business has been consistently increasing. For example, at the beginning of 2019, the number of bitcoin ATMs alone exceeded 4000, and every day at least seven new devices are installed throughout the world. Moreover, no less than one-third of all existing ATMs not only offer cash for bitcoins, but can also perform a reverse operation to purchase cryptocurrency. More than one-half of all bitcoin ATMs in the world are installed in the United States, but other countries are gradually increasing their number, with especially positive trends in Canada and Austria. In total, there are more than three dozen manufacturers of such ATMs, and the cost of one machine is about USD 10,000.

One of the obstacles hindering the mass distribution of cryptocurrencies is their virtuality. For many people accustomed to dealing with coins and banknotes, an intangible form of money is unusual – not to mention the relative technological complexity of using them to pay for goods and services. Physical money is often held as a collector's item, which could hardly be possible for cryptocurrencies. However, in 2011, a certain Mike Caldwell decided to issue collectible bitcoins in the form of physical coins. He designed a metal coin denominated in bitcoins. Each coin corresponded to a crypto wallet containing a number of bitcoins equivalent to the denomination of the coin. In this case, the secret key of the wallet was printed onto the coin itself in the form of a code and covered with a special hologram, which, if necessary, could be destroyed to gain access to the key and the funds in the wallet. Obviously, once the hologram was destroyed, the coin lost virtually all of its utility, since the key ceased to be secret to anyone who could see the coin.

Several thousand of these coins were issued, almost all of which were bought up by collectors and cryptoenthusiasts. Subsequently, there were attempts by other manufacturers to create coins denominated in bitcoins, including large denominations, but they failed to come into widespread use.

For the sake of objectivity, it is necessary to consider the drawbacks of using bitcoin as a means of payment. We are talking about one of its most important properties: anonymity. Indeed, the untraceability of cryptocurrency payments and the technological inability to link the transaction with the individual directly responsible has led to the emergence of an entire criminal industry offering various illegal goods and services with payment exclusively in cryptocurrencies. Many national governments view the emergence and existence of this kind of activity as one of the main factors preventing cryptocurrencies – and in particular bitcoin – from obtaining the status of an official means of payment. Now, let us turn to the immediate history of the question.

In 2011, a website called Silk Road appeared on the internet. This trading portal made it possible to purchase a wide range of illegal goods and services – drugs, stolen bank cards, counterfeit money, and even the services of a hit man. In order to ensure the anonymity of buyers and sellers, the site solely accepted payment in bitcoins. The owner of the site was a certain Ross Ulbricht, a resident of the United States, professing extreme political views that deny any form of government interference in peoples' lives. In 2012–2013, the annual sales volume of the site was estimated at about USD 12–15 million, and the total volume of transactions in the cryptocurrency equivalent was close to 10 million bitcoins. In total, about 100, 000 buyers and sellers managed to use the services of the site. Ulbricht was eventually arrested and received a lifetime sentence in 2015, and the Silk Road website was shut down. Nevertheless, the very appearance and existence of such a service remained a blemish on the reputation of bitcoin as a means of making anonymous payments on the internet. Numerous government officials and regulators around the world have since cited this story as an example and explanation of why the recognition of cryptocurrencies as an official means of payment is premature – if not entirely unacceptable.

In defense of digital money, the counterargument can be made that many useful everyday items can also be used not only for their intended purpose, but also for explicitly criminal purposes. For example, kitchen knives have become an instrument of crime on countless occasions. However, they have never been legally prohibited from being sold and used for cutting groceries in kitchens around the world. Similarly, ordinary banknotes are routinely used to commit crimes – primarily in cases involving corruption. However, this has never been seen as a reason to complete withdraw them from circulation in favor of other forms of payment. This begs the logical conclusion that the possible criminal use of a number of household items is a natural consequence of their very existence. Nonetheless, banning them would do human civilization more harm than good. As such, a similarly balanced approach should be applied in the case of cryptocurrencies. Instead of overarching bans, it would be necessary to fight against the possible illegal use of digital currencies with the aid of professional state services.

Concluding the section devoted to Bitcoin, I would like to note once again that this project has become a pioneer in the cutting-edge high-tech industry of blockchain. Since its appearance, almost ten years have passed, and many in the cryptocurrency industry quite logically consider Bitcoin to be somewhat outdated and no longer up to the challenges of the modern day. But thanks to such critics, Bitcoin began to have competitors. By the beginning of 2019, there were already more than 2000 different cryptocurrencies in the blockchain industry with at least one stock valuation. Admittedly, most of these projects will remain outside the scope of this book's inquiry. However, we will focus on the most significant of the so-called "altcoins" – cryptocurrencies which are an alternative to Bitcoin. Each of these projects attempted to create some unique value proposition that distinguishes it from its "forebear." The first such project that we will consider is the Ethereum project, which is sometimes called Bitcoin 2.0 due to the fact that it took the blockchain technology to the next stage of its development.

Introduction to Ethereum

After about five years since the appearance of the Bitcoin network – the first system to be created on the basis of blockchain technology – a decent number of projects had already come into circulation in the as-yet nascent crypto industry. To a large degree, most of them were "bitcoin-like" and differed from their prototype only in superficial minutiae. However, just as with the Bitcoin project itself, most of its subsequent clones essentially offered more of the same: run-of-the-mill decentralized payment systems which remained rather rudimentary in their capabilities. Nevertheless, having taken stock of all the advantages of blockchain technology, the emerging blockchain industry began to exhibit a demand for blockchain networks with more complex functionality. The crypto community had appreciated the need for more advanced technological means in order to start building decentralized projects at a qualitatively new level.

At the end of 2013, such a tool was indeed proposed by a cryptoenthusiast known to the community at that time as the editor of *Bitcoin Magazine*. It was Vitalik Buterin, a 19-year-old Russian-Canadian programmer, who presented a description of the Ethereum project whose capabilities drew heightened attention. Ethereum put forth completely new concepts – far beyond the potential of the typical blockchain projects. Moreover, this project was not positioned as a payment system at all, but was actually a new generation blockchain platform. The most important innovation was the system of so-called "smart contracts." We will take a look at the structure and principles of smart contracts at a later point, whereas for now we will outline the main properties which set the Ethereum project apart from Bitcoin and similar systems.

Let's start with how addresses are generated. Just like in the Bitcoin project, Ethereum uses a similar algorithm to create them, but does not convert them to a more "legible" form, leaving the hash of the public key virtually unmodified. In part, this was done also because Ethereum, as mentioned above, was not originally conceived as a payment system. Therefore, in this system they did not try to generate addresses with greater "presentability," thus simplifying the process of manual entry. In addition to the differences in the generation of addressing, the project creators decided that the blocks in the system will be created much faster than in the Bitcoin network. In this case, their size will be limited not by the number of bytes, but by the required computing power for processing the block data. Such measures proved indeed to be a clever idea because the presence of smart contracts, as we will see in their more detailed study, actually obliges developers to introduce such limits.

Mining in the Ethereum network differs significantly from the operating principles of Bitcoin, despite the fact that it also uses the proof-of-work principle to find blocks. Also, as with Bitcoin, management of the complexity of the computational problem depends on the total network hash rate. However, the degree of complexity is significantly reduced, so it takes much less time to create an Ethereum block. At the moment, the average time to create a block in the Ethereum network is about thirteen seconds – as compared to ten minutes in the Bitcoin network. In other words, in the time necessary for creating one block in the Bitcoin network, nearly fifty are built in the Ethereum network. As a result, the base of blocks and transactions in the Ethereum network is already comparable to that of Bitcoin, despite the fact that Ethereum appeared six and a half years after Bitcoin – the pioneer of blockchain projects. Payments within the network, including the payment of transaction fees and mining compensation are made in a cryptocurrency called "ether." In cases where the complexity of finding a valid hash during mining is relatively low, blocks in the network are created quite quickly. This means that the value of the reward for mining is proportionally small and completely incomparable in value with the premium for creating blocks in the Bitcoin network.

In our description of the principles of decentralized mining in the Bitcoin network, we considered the conflict scenario that could arise if different nodes find blocks within a ten-minute time interval. The resulting branches in the block chain must ultimately be discarded by the network in favor of the longer chain. The Ethereum network employs a similar principle. However, due to the fact that its blocks are generated with nearly fifty times the speed, scenarios with competing blocks being found also occur about fifty times as often. Therefore, the Ethereum network is in quasi-perpetual state of having alternative chains that threaten the integrity of the network, so it is constantly faced with the necessity of having to opt for the branch which presents greater value for the system. For this purpose, Ethereum uses the Greedy Heaviest Observed Subtree (GHOST) protocol which gives preference to branches with blocks which took the most calculations to extract.

Given that competing blocks are often created almost simultaneously, the question of how to reward miners arises. If you reward a single miner as the winner, this could significantly motivate everyone else who also found a block. Since the miners competing with one another are performing equally complex computational work, the system creators to allocate a portion of the reward for a maximum of two blocks found in parallel without being accepted by the network. Such blocks are called "uncles" because they have a common "ancestor block." The miners who create them also receive a certain bonus, albeit less for creating a block accepted by the network as true; for this purpose, there is a special formula for distributing the reward.

The actual procedure of mining ether also differs from the Bitcoin project. Ethereum uses a completely different algorithm to search for valid hashes, which the developers named Ethash. The extreme electricity consumption required for bitcoin mining has always been an issue of concern for Ethereum founder Buterin. Therefore, he decided to combat the excessive increase in the total hash rate in his project – primarily via the use of ASIC devices for mining. As such, the decision was made to complicate the algorithm for searching through hashes to a level at which it would require significantly more RAM than the SHA-256 algorithm used in the Bitcoin network.

As you know, large-scale miners amass hefty amounts of computational power by constructing farms comprised of ASIC devices. The presence of farms is considered a negative factor for any blockchain network, as mining thus takes on a more centralized nature. In turn, this contradicts the originally conceived plan of using network management to eliminate any points where computing power could be excessively consolidated – to the greatest possible extent. In one of his many interviews Buterin told the story that at a very young age he spent a lot of time playing the popular computer game World of Warcraft. From time to time, his virtual character lost his abilities due to the correction of the game balance, which was periodically carried out by the Blizzard developers, without taking into account the opinion of the gaming community. Each time that the game rules were thus changed, the young man would experience a strong emotional shock due to the fact that his personal efforts to develop his character had been essentially nullified. Moreover, the decisions had been made by a centralized body over which he could not exert any influence. Apparently, these psychological scars from childhood had a considerable impact on the future world view of Buterin, who concluded that centralized management represents an absolute evil.

Despite the measures taken by Buterin to bolster the memory requirements for mining, he unfortunately did not manage to entirely keep ASIC devices from emerging on the Ethereum network. However, he did manage to significantly reduce the hash rate of such devices for mining cryptocoins and, consequently, to ensure greater decentralization of mining, thus making it thus more competitive. If we compare two mining devices for the Bitcoin and Ethereum network, we will see that for the extraction of ether, the miner sorts out hashes tens of thousands of times slower than its bitcoin counterpart. This is because when mining ether, the Ethash algorithm requires constantly accessing the RAM memory, which has additional information necessary for the correct operation of mining procedures. These frequent calls slow down the algorithm so much that the difference in the speed of the hash iteration is at least four orders of magnitude.

This approach also made it possible to preserve the possibility of mining ether coins with conventional graphics card processors, thereby guaranteeing much greater decentralization of the process of finding new Ethereum blocks. Overall, the entire Ethereum network consumes almost three times less electricity than the Bitcoin network, although level of consumption is still quite considerable. Therefore, the developers of the Ethereum project remain legitimately concerned about the energy intensity of their project and plan to radically reconsider the principles of creating blocks in the network in the near future. Currently, the Ethereum network is in the process of phasing out mining based on the proof-of-work consensus protocol in favor of the proof-of-stake principle, which we will cover separately at a later point.

As for the basic unit of calculation in Ethereum, the ether – in contrast to bitcoin, which can be divided into 100 million parts (i.e. eight decimal places) – is divided into a quintillion parts – i.e. as much as 18 decimal places. The smallest unit of the ether is called a Wei in honor of Wei Dai, the creator of the B-money project, and one-millionth of the ether is named Szabo in honor of Nick Szabo, the inventor of smart contracts and the author of the BitGold project which is considered the most similar to the Bitcoin project itself. Finally, one-thousandth of the ether was named Finney in honor of Hal Finney, one of the developers of the cryptographic PGP protocol and Satoshi Nakamoto's counterparty on the very first bitcoin transaction in January 2009.

Another important difference to bitcoins is that at present, the issue of ether is not specifically limited and, thus, could be subject to inflation in the future. When Vitalik Buterin presented his project, he simultaneously created and sold to investors about 60 million ether coins, thus fetching about USD

18.5 million in return for them. Buterin placed about 12 million ether coins in reserve to finance further development of the project in the future. Such a one-time issue of coins is usually called "pre-mining."

The platform itself was launched on July 30, 2015. Since then, over the past nearly four years, with the help of already conventional mining procedures, slightly more than 30 million coins have been issued. Thus, their total number has exceeded 100 million with a total current capitalization of just under USD 20 billion. In terms of popularity, ether has a firm hold on second place in the cryptocurrency industry trailing only bitcoin and are traded on almost all exchanges which offer cryptocurrency trading services. If bitcoin is commonly called "the gold of cryptocurrency," ether received the honor of "silver."

Over half a million transactions are made in the global Ethereum network on a daily basis. If we look at the principle of accounting for the balances of coins held on system addresses, then there is another important difference from the Bitcoin network. As you know, blockchain transactions are chains of electronic signatures that can be traced throughout the database of blocks. In this way, the balance of any of the addresses can be automatically calculated by matching its inputs as income and outputs as expenditures. The total of unspent outputs will be the current balance of the address. This principle is called UTXO – i.e. accounting for unspent transactional outputs – and we've already spent some time considering it. The Ethereum network decided that it would be advisable to maintain a database of current statuses for each of the network addresses. Although this method of accounting requires the additional storage of a certain amount of data, it offers incomparably greater convenience than the UTXO principle, which requires the constant performance of calculations to obtain the up-to-date status of addresses.

At the same time, the principle of storing current statuses made it possible for developers to introduce the unique functionality of smart contracts to the Ethereum platform from its very inception, which indeed comprised the project's primary value proposition. What are smart contracts and what impact did their implementation in the Ethereum network have on the development of blockchain technology in general?

Smart contracts

Throughout the process of introducing new technologies, the developers of systems using bitcoins as a means of payment constantly encountered the problem of creating more complex models of carrying out transactions – especially systems that might have any non-standard conditions. Satoshi Nakamoto attempted to make provisions for such a scenario and, starting with the first version of the software implementation of the bitcoin network client and gave it a so-called script system for processing transactions. In fact, it was a simplified form of a stack-type programming language, where all its commands are processed in a left-to-right order of how they were specified in the script itself.

The script language of Bitcoin contains about eight dozen different commands, each of which performs a certain algorithmic operation, ranging from elementary tasks (e.g. comparing two numeric values) to more complex ones (e.g. hashing data or algorithms to verify a digital electronic signature). In the vast majority of cases, the output parameters for each transaction fits a standard script called or Pay to Public Key Hash (P2PKH). This script implements the payment procedure on the hash of the public key, which, in fact, is the bitcoin address of the transaction recipient.

To handle non-standard payment situations, the sender can create their own script which contains additional conditions for processing the transaction. That said, the options are admittedly not numerous. For example, it is possible to implement the multi-signature functionality or specify in the script a time period prior to which the transferred funds may not be spent. However, such means offer nearly no scope for implementing truly sophisticated algorithmic constructions for processing transactions with an additional set of parameters. Plus, the main issue is not that the set of commands is limited in the bitcoin script, but rather that this language fails to satisfy the condition of Turing completeness. What does that mean?

In 1936, Alan Turing, the future hero of the cryptographic war with Enigma, the German encryption device, proposed a model of the computer in the form of a mathematical abstraction. The resulting model was later called the "Turing Machine." This logical computational design served as a tool to prove the presence or absence of an algorithmic solution for various problems. As for "Turing completeness," one of its criteria is the presence in the programming language of commands which can be used to build algorithmic cycles. The script language of the bitcoin network does not provide commands for loop processing, which vastly restricts the possibilities of using it to implement complex computational algorithms. Unlike Bitcoin, the Ethereum project provides for this possibility, and this is precisely where the smart contracts function comes into play. Let's take a look at what they offer.

As has been repeatedly mentioned, the concept was first developed by Nick Szabo, who first presented the form of executable electronic contracts in a decentralized environment in 1994. Szabo defined this type of virtual agreement as "an information transfer protocol that ensures the automatic execution of the transaction terms by the parties." In Szabo's view, the advantages of this concept of contracting included: confidentiality, low transaction costs, and the absence of the need for intermediaries to ensure the parties' confidence. If we compare electronic contracts with conventional ones, an apparent difference lies in the ability of a smart contract to control only mathematically provable terms of the transaction, whereas a conventional may contain terms which are vague or descriptive. Ultimately, Nick Szabo never went further than a theoretical representation of his model, and it was not for another two decades that a direct application of this concept came to fruition in the Ethereum project.

Generally speaking, the process of setting up a smart contract is similar to a normal transaction, which contains a number of additional elements that give it unique properties. First and foremost, we are talking about the program code, which is subject to decentralized execution via direct use of the "Ethereum virtual machine" (EVM) on the network nodes creating the blocks. The code of the smart contract describes the algorithmic logic of processing transactions between network users and the owner of the smart contract, who placed it in the blockchain, thus granting it validity. From this point on, the smart contract is present in one of the blocks of the chain, and any network participant can activate its operation by sending a transaction to the contract address in the system. As such, the smart contract is a network subject in its own right with the ability to accept and form transactions. Yet, it cannot do so independently, but rather only when the contract code is executed by the EVM on the miner's node when creating a new block. How does this process transpire?

For the sake of simplicity, a smart contract can be compared to a vending machine that sells, for example, drinks. Whether by cash or bank card, the buyer makes appropriate payment, and the machine dispenses the selected product in accordance with the deposited funds. If this situation is projected onto the blockchain network, the smart contract is activated at the moment when a transaction is placed in the block and sends some cryptocurrency assets to the address of the contact. When processing such a transaction, the miner finds the block that contains the smart contract and using the virtual machine executes its code for processing, thus giving it transaction data for "input." Depending on the logic of the algorithm embedded in the code itself, the smart contract can have different results. This can be simply a change in the system status or response transactions set up by the contract – one or even more. We should also not forget that smart contracts can be launched not only by miners, but also by ordinary nodes. This happens when they process transactions related to smart contracts, including when performing validity checks on blocks received from miners. On the one hand, such a protocol entails some computational redundancy while also providing an additional guarantee of system-level stability.

Unlike the bitcoin script language, smart contracts are coded in programming languages which meet the Turing completeness criteria. The language most commonly used in Ethereum smart contracts is the object-oriented language Solidity, which is semantically similar to the popular programming language JavaScript. However, the body of the smart contract does not directly contain source code written, for example, in Solidity, but rather a version of it which has undergone compiling – i.e. so-called "bytecode." This code is a compact set of low-level commands designed to be executed by an EVM.

In a decentralized blockchain system where each block and each transaction can be analyzed by any participant of the network, Ethereum smart contracts are no exception. However, since the contract is stored in bytecode format in the blockchain database, special decompilers are employed to make sense of its operating principles. These are programs convert the code into a relatively "legible" form, albeit one still quite far removed from the source code – as originally created by the smart contract programmer. The decompiler can neither restore the original names of variables nor the comments that the programmer left on the code. For this reason, it becomes difficult to reproduce the original logic of the algorithm once the smart contract code has been decompiled. There are, however, reverse situations, when the creators of smart contracts publish the source code to ensure greater transparency and confidence in their algorithms. These are published on external internet resources, where readers can acquaint themselves with the code text in an easy-to-read form containing the necessary comments.

Like any ordinary computer program, a smart contract has various functionalities. As such, some smart contracts require only a few lines of code, while others can be complex algorithms consisting of hundreds or even thousands of lines. Above all, this suggests that as concerns the amount of computational effort required, smart contracts are far from being entirely identical to one another – they can each require different amounts of CPU time. Quite logically, this gives rise to the following question: how should incentives be structured for miners that process such contracts? What if the smart contract code contains, for example, an infinite loop that puts the processor's computer into a "hanging" state, where it endlessly attempts to loop through the same set of operations? As a measure of prophylaxis against such scenarios, Ethereum provides a model of compensating for computing power with the help of a special "fuel" for processing smart contracts. In the Ethereum community, this type of "fuel" is referred to as "gas."

Oddly enough, the main cryptocurrency used for payment in the Ethereum network – ether – was created primarily for a most important utilitarian purpose: to pay for gas to process smart contracts. Gas itself is a countable, but non-monetary value and directly reflects the amount of computational resources spent by the miner to execute the smart contract code. For every command in the Ethereum bytecode, there is a fixed "cost" denominated in units of gas. Simple commands like arithmetic operations cost less, whereas complex procedures (e.g. hashing) are more costly. In other words, the system originally contained the equivalent of a price list which could be used to calculate how much gas would be required to process a given smart contract. Since conventional transactions for transferring cryptocurrency from one destination to another also require computational processing, then they also have their own equivalent "gas price." Typically, a standard transaction costs 21,000 gas, the only question is how much the gas itself costs.

The price of gas constantly fluctuates depending on the current load on the Ethereum network. If the queue of transactions requiring processing and inclusion in the block starts to back up, miners prioritize the transactions where the senders have specified a higher gas price. Before the first version of the Ethereum client was launched, it was established that a unit of gas would cost 10,000 Gwei or a single one-hundred-thousandth of ether. Currently, this price would be considered extremely high, as the price of ether has skyrocketed since the time of the project's launch – albeit still quite far from its historical peak. Nonetheless, if you purchase gas at this price, then the cost of sending a normal transaction today is about USD 30.

Obviously, as the price of ether increased, the price of gas fell proportionately except for brief periods when the network load drastically spiked. In this case, people sending transactions vied for priority inclusion in the next blocks to be created by boosting the gas price. In the spring of 2019, the average gas price hovered between 2–4 Gwei which makes an average transaction fee the rough equivalent of one or two cents on the US dollar. When sending a transaction, you can specify a lower gas price than the current market price. In this case, the transaction will require a longer processing time than usual, and if the price is set much lower than the market rate, the transaction risks not being processed at all.

When sending a transaction to the network for interaction with a smart contract, the sender can only approximate how much gas will be required to process it. Therefore, no exact value of the gas is specified, but rather a value with an upper limit – i.e. the maximum amount of gas that it is willing to allow to "burn" for its transaction. The exact value will be set by the miner during the direct processing of the transaction and the smart contract, and the sender will be charged exactly the amount actually spent, whereupon the unused balance will be refunded to their account. In the event that the specified gas limit for processing the smart contract proves insufficient, its implementation will be prematurely terminated and the "deal" will not take place. In this case, the gas already used will not be returned, and its cost will be credited to the miner as income.

If you analyze all the transactions in a block, including those related to smart contracts, you can calculate the total amount of gas required to process the entire block. Accordingly, the block size in the Ethereum network is not limited to a certain number of bytes as in Bitcoin, but rather by a maximum permissible amount of gas per block. As such, a block may contain a small number of transactions which are exceedingly "gas-intensive," and the limit is thus reached quite quickly. At the moment, the limit for one block is about 8 million units of gas, which permits nearly 400 standard-sized transactions to be placed in one Ethereum block. Presumably, the gas limit per block will grow along with the natural increase in the computational capabilities of the network nodes.

Now, it is starting to become clear why the concept of smart contracts has a number of obvious advantages over conventional contracts. Yet, one should not overlook the fact that they also come with vulnerabilities. Network participants are the ones who set up the smart contracts, which indelibly imparts a "human factor" to the process. As example of such would be the professional qualification of programmers who develop the algorithms and program codes. Throughout the several years of the Ethereum project's existence, there have been many cases when mistakes made by programmers when writing codes for smart contracts led to serious financial losses.

Critical evaluations often account for such when assessing such systems, as the full openness and decentralization of the network make it difficult to fully prevent. In February 2018, a consolidated group of experts announced that about 34,000 smart contracts in the Ethereum network have potential problems and vulnerabilities of which their owners as yet are unaware. In some cases, errors in the codes of smart contracts have been exploited by attackers to steal tens of millions of dollars. In order to minimize risks, authors of smart contracts are recommended to devote more time to their testing, as well as to enlist code audit services from recognized industry professionals.

The time has finally come to consider the primary functions currently performed by smart contracts in the Ethereum network. According to statistics, just under 2 million smart contracts have been placed in the network, with about 500,000 presently having the status of "active." The total number of transactions involving smart contracts is estimated at more than 100 million. A certain part of smart contracts provided for the activities of decentralized cryptocurrency exchanges, support for over-the-counter transactions between counterparties, as well as the organization of cryptogames, some of which have gained widespread popularity. Yet the vast majority of smart contracts have been used to ensure the issue and circulation of so-called digital "tokens." In fact, it was the Ethereum project itself that introduced the fascinating and exceptionally far-reaching phenomenon called "tokenization" to the digital decentralized world, but in order to do any justice to the details, this will need to be a story of its own.

Tokenization

Each blockchain platform has its main cryptocurrency in the form of digital coins. The need to issue its own cryptocurrency is usually dictated by the need to create monetary incentive for the nodes that support the stable operation of the network. In particular, the Bitcoin and Ethereum projects have their own core cryptocurrencies, which are used for the payment of both mining and transaction fees. In addition, these cryptocurrencies are also used as means of payment and even as instruments for investment. It should be stated, however, that the original concept of the Ethereum project did not provide for such use of its coins, but it developed as a natural consequence of the project's capabilities. The Ethereum offered decentralized projects the possibilities to create their own digital assets, and this type of assets began to be called digital crypto tokens or simply tokens. The main difference between tokens and coins is the absence of their own blockchain infrastructure; instead, they represented a technological add-on to the existing network, which ensured their emission and decentralized circulation.

Why would developers of projects based on the Ethereum network need their own tokens, and why did they not want to use the network's existing cryptocurrency – ether – for their needs? First of all, they did not want to find themselves dependent on the market conditions of the price of ether, as this could fluctuate quite significantly. Indeed, subsequent events proved these concerns to be well-founded. But the main reason was the fact that ether simply did not suit the needs of nearly all the projects, as their requirements extended beyond the usual properties of cryptocoins. Many projects saw themselves faced with the need to create a new type of digital assets, radically different from the typical core cryptocurrencies used as a means of payment. Now, we will take a closer look at these differences.

Generally speaking, tokens should be considered as a unit of account. That said, this does not necessarily have to represent digital money (even if crypto tokens have become most famous in this capacity). Quite a few projects have integrated special payment tokens into their systems with its own ascribed internal value which is not subject to fluctuations in the price of ether. These tokens are referred to as "utility" tokens and served as either internal money for their projects or other forms of accounting units – e.g. loyalty program points of some company or something similar. Utility tokens are intended for a single primary purpose – to serve as a means of settlement for the goods or services offered by the projects. They are not security-backed assets, and theoretically speaking, their market value should not depend on the success or failure of the project. In reality, however, the volume of demand for utility tokens does impact their market price, and the amount of demand itself is a function of the popularity of the particular crypto project offering its tokens for implementation.

When creating their projects, developers are often desperately strapped for investments. Quite rarely do they manage to cover all the costs of creating a project on their own, which would not be unfeasible for a larger corporation with its own financial reserves. For this reason, a group of programmer enthusiasts who have developed an interesting idea for their project are more prone to try drumming up external financing in the early stages of the project. Crypto projects based on blockchain technology have found issuing their own tokens to be an excellent way of pooling considerable funds for development. This process is called an "initial coin offering" (ICO) – by analogy with the well-known term "initial public offering" (IPO), when prior to entering the stock exchange, a company issues shares and thus attracts funds for further development.

If any project presents the tokens issued not as a utilitarian means for payments internal to the created system, but as virtual shares of its own company, then we are talking about a completely different type of token as a digital asset. It is necessary to take into account the fact that when an investor acquires such tokens, they, in theory, should become a co-owner of the issuing company and receive, therewith, all related privileges, including dividends from its activities and the right to vote on important decisions. For now, the legal aspect of this discussion will remain outside the purview of our discussion. For now, it suffices to note that in this case we are dealing with so-called "security" tokens, which are designed to reflect the legal right of ownership by the purchaser of a proportional portion of the project.

Project owners use smart contracts to conduct procedures for the initial placement of tokens in the Ethereum network. They put together the contract code in such a way that upon receiving from any investor any amount denominated in ether, they are given in exchange the appropriate number of project tokens, depending on the conditions of placement. In this case, the smart contract oversees the issue and distribution of tokens. If project owners want to, for example, encourage early acquisition of their tokens, they can set lower prices for them according to the date of investment. In this case, the smart contract must process the current date and compare it with the discount table in the conditions, thus determining the token price for the current time period. In the same way, a smart contract can also buy tokens from investors at the price declared by the contract owners, accepting tokens and issuing in exchange the appropriate amount of ether. There are also cases when you need to dispose of unnecessary tokens by "burning" them – e.g. sending them to a non-existent address in the network, to which none of the participants has a secret key.

Regrettably, many owners of crypto projects often fail to call attention to the fundamental differences between the types of tokens that they offer to investors for sale. In the cryptocurrency industry, there are cases when under the auspices of the ICO, no security tokens were being distributed, but rather only utility tokens – i.e. which did not impart any ownership right. Such precedents quickly attracted the attention of financial regulators in various countries, who actively undertook work on statutory distinctions between types of tokens, while simultaneously making their differences clear to investors. It should come as no surprise that national entities adopted their own individual stances on this new form of acquiring capital. Some countries hurried to create a most-favored-nation regime for projects conducting ICOs and quickly made appropriate changes and additions to their national legislation. Others took a wait-and-see attitude, not daring to take drastic measures in one direction or the other. Some jurisdictions immediately adopted a negative stance on such processes and even applied a number of measures aimed at curbing the local crypto industry, obliging project owners to return the ICO funds to investors.

Although utility and security tokens dominate the crypto industry as a whole, the list of types of digital tokens goes far beyond these two examples. There is every reason to believe that tokenization's brightest prospects lie in "digitalization" or the conversion of ordinary financial assets into digital form. These include fiat currencies, corporate shares, commodities, or derivatives such as futures, options, or contracts for difference. For each of these financial assets, there is an opportunity to issue tokens that will circulate in decentralized blockchain environments with all the concomitant benefits. Such tokens would have a number of features. First of all, their price would depend entirely on fluctuations in the market value of the "underlying asset" in the classical financial markets. In other words, their price should always be stable relative to their underlying assets – hence, the choice to dub this type of token a "stablecoin."

The second important distinction from utility tokens is the need to set up mechanisms to fully back the stablecoin with the relevant underlying assets. Implementation of such models would certainly require a centralized approach – i.e. by means of special depositaries entrusted with the safekeeping of the necessary amounts of basic security. Depositaries of this type should take custody of the underlying asset and give the user in exchange the appropriate stablecoin. The same also applies in reverse: when the depositary takes back the stablecoins, they undertake to exchange them for an equal amount of the underlying asset in custody. To illustrate the point, we can have a look at the Tether project, which issues stablecoins of the US dollar in the Ethereum and Bitcoin networks (via the OmniLayer platform).

Tether was released in 2015 by the Hong Kong company Tether Limited, which undertook to guarantee the issuing and the backing. The tokenization of the dollar arose in response to considerable demand from individuals trading on cryptocurrency exchanges, who wanted to exchange cryptocurrencies not only for each other, but also for digital substitutes for fiat currencies. In so doing, they sought to protect themselves from fluctuations in the price of cryptocurrencies by temporarily placing their funds into the equivalent of a fiat currency. Also, many of them just wanted to convert the cryptocurrencies into dollar tokens and then redeem them directly with the issuer in exchange for ordinary dollars, which would be paid out to them via bank transfer from the funds held in custody.

It would be logical to presume that if a company issues, say, USD 1 million stablecoins, then its bank account holds an equivalent amount in physical dollars to back the tokens. However, the mechanisms for securing stablecoins with underlying assets lie outside the framework of the blockchain network as such and represent a centralized service founded on trust. As such, it is incumbent on the issuer to assure sufficient transparency in its dealings. In the case of Tether, the depositary was clearly lacking in transparency. The company has never agreed to external financial audits, and meanwhile as at the spring of 2019, the total issue of USDT tokens (Tether) exceeded USD 2.5 billion. Not so surprisingly, the company is under the constant scrutiny of financial regulators both in Hong Kong and the United States (the entity issuing dollars!), where regulators in 2018 banned the company's operations with national residents. That notwithstanding, Tether stablecoins continue to enjoy exceptional popularity among crypto traders, and they have no problems with trust – if only for now.

Despite the organizational and regulatory difficulties of tokenizing classical financial assets, this process is gradually gaining popularity. There are projects that offer tokenization of precious metals or stock exchange companies. In addition to the Ethereum network, other tokenizing platforms have begun to appear on the market, but it is not easy for them to compete with the industry leader which consolidates the overwhelming majority of issued tokens. In order to lend industry tokenization a systemic form, the Ethereum project has developed special standards for various types of tokens. At present, the most popular standard is ERC-20, the format used by most projects to issue their various tokens. This standard lays down a set of technical specifications for issued tokens to ensure their network-wide acceptance, compatibility with other tokens in the system, and their seamless integration into the system.

Quite often, token holders need to exchange one token for another. In its fundamental form, the Ethereum network does not permit different tokens to be exchanged within a single transaction. Instead, this requires a minimum of two transactions in the form of a counter transaction. Since all transactions in blockchain networks are "irrevocable," in such cases the issue of ensuring trust between the parties takes on heightened relevance. The most popular method of exchange is cryptocurrency exchanges, which host the vast majority of transactions with tokens, including the ERC-20 standard. There also exists a number of decentralized exchanges that specialize exclusively in the exchange of Ethereum network tokens among themselves.

In the not-even four years of Ethereum's existence, it has issued slightly less than 200,000 tokens of various types – utility, security, and a number of others. Such a scale of tokenization suggests that the cryptocurrency industry is developing robustly, and in the near future we will be able to see more and more projects built around this type of digital assets. According to some estimates, the industry of decentralized applications based on the Ethereum platform employs hundreds of thousands of IT professionals around the world, and this number is only moving upwards The capabilities of the Ethereum network itself are also expanding: its developers and, above all, Vitalik Buterin himself are constantly on the lookout for ways to improve the network and address the issues that inevitably arise throughout the course of the project's work. Examples of such include the excessive growth of the size of the base blocks, and, of course, the amount of electricity spent on mining. Currently, the Ethereum network is in a state of transition from the energy-intensive type of proof-of-work consensus to a more progressive algorithm that will slash the exceptional energy costs as it operates according to a completely different principle. It is called proof-of-stake and is already being widely used in a number of crypto projects. As the primary alternative to the proof-of-work algorithm, this principle has gradually begun replacing its energy-inefficient competitor.

Proof-of-stake

When analyzing the principles of protection of blockchain networks using the proof-of-work algorithm, both its advantages and disadvantages are explicitly outlined. Clearly to its credit is the mathematical rigor with which the computational problem is formulated; indeed, solving this problem gives an undeniable right to a reward for the creation of the block. Alongside that, however there are also negative aspects: the elevated energy costs. Moreover, these are used quite irrationally, since the results obtained from the calculation forfeit their benefit once a new block starts being created. For understandable reasons, this method of achieving consensus in decentralized environments receives its fair share of critical feedback related to the inefficient use of energy resources. Since the early days of the Bitcoin network, this issue has caused concern among cryptoenthusiasts who foresaw in their calculations that the total energy consumption of the entire network would grow along with the popularity of the crypto project. This problem was seriously discussed by the crypto community, when in July 2011, at one of the most popular Bitcoin forums, a revolutionary idea was voiced that energy-dependent mining could become a relic of the past. As a replacement for the concept of proof of work, a "proof-of-ownership" model was proposed, which has since been called proof-of-stake.

Masked behind the forum pseudonym QuantumMechanic, the author of the idea stated that the potential of owning a cryptocurrency could be used instead of contributing computing power to the network nodes, as is done with conventional mining. In other words, they proposed giving the right to create blocks to nodes, which had held a significantly positive balance of cryptocoins for a relatively long time. The idea was fully supported and developed by the crypto community. About a year later, in August 2012, developers Scott Nadal and Sunny King introduced the Peercoin payment system. It was the first blockchain network to bolster the standard proof-of-work principle with proof-of-stake elements, thus creating a hybrid consensus mechanism. The proof-of-work (PoW) Protocol in the Peercoin network was used to generate new monetary issues in the form of rewards for miners creating blocks, along with transaction fees – similar to the Bitcoin network. However, blocks that were created on the basis of the proof-of-stake (PoS) principle could also appear alongside the PoW blocks in the network.

Creating a block required carrying out actions that bore a faint resemblance to mining. Only now the creators of PoS blocks were not called miners, but validators – i.e. nodes that confirm blocks. The process of creating the block was called forging or minting. Before a new block could be created, the validator had to what amount of cryptocoins they possessed. As with mining, certain parameters had to be hashed, such as the data of the previous block, the current time, and the address where the funds belonging to the validator were located. The resulting hash was compared with the product of two values, which represented the number of coins in the validator's possession and how long they had been there. As soon as a hash was obtained smaller in value than this product, the block was considered created. Obviously, the more coins the validator has and the longer they have owned them, the higher the chances that the product of these numbers will be very large and exceed the randomly generated hash, which can simply be viewed as a normal number. Since there is only one constantly changing parameter in the process of hashing – the time in seconds expressed as a whole integer – the hash itself can change only once per second. The validator who created the block did not receive a direct reward for this, but rather earned only a cumulative fee from the transactions which they placed in the block.

As follows from the algorithm for creating PoS blocks, significant energy consumption is not required. However, this does not mean that this type of consensus is devoid of drawbacks or disadvantages. In fact, a validator that creates blocks on the principle of PoS freezes the funds in their account and forgoes the right to use them for a long time, so as not to forfeit the accumulated potential for the possible creation of blocks. For the network itself, this is not exceptionally desirable because the speed of money circulating within it can significantly slow down, which will have a negative impact on the possibilities for its use and development. This method of creating blocks gives nodes incentive to primarily accumulate, rather than spend their funds. In such a scenario, excessive consolidation under the control of one or more nodes can – contrary to the original notion – increase the degree to which network management processes are centralized. Also, nodes which own a relatively small share of cryptocurrencies find themselves relatively sidelined from the process of creating blocks, since they have virtually no chance of become validators due to their insignificant financial potential.

To eliminate these drawbacks, a modification of the PoS protocol was developed, which introduced mechanisms for delegating the authority of validators from ordinary network participants to nodes which they had selected. By means of a special transaction, each node can vote in favor of one or more potential validator candidates. The delegate nodes that get the most votes may not have a significant amount of coins, but they are willing to contribute their computing power to maintain the stability of the network and receive in exchange a relatively modest transaction fee. This principle has been called "delegated PoS" (DPoS), and it is this form of PoS protocol that subsequently became most widely used in projects that decided to abandon the energy-intensive proof-of-work algorithm.

The difference between DPoS and the classical form of PoS is that the validators, who received the right to delegate, no longer iterate over the hashes to find a suitable value. Instead, they form a queue of similar delegates to agree on a strict order of block generation. Each of the validators is allocated a certain time period during which they have the right to create a block to be accepted by the entire network. The period itself can be quite short and measured in units of seconds, depending on the network protocol and how much bandwidth the network participants want to receive for their transactions. If for some reason the validator missed their turn, the right to create a block passes to the next validator in line. The order itself has standardized rules of formation, and each validator performs the calculations independently. Understandably, this calculated order must be a precise match for all the validators as failure to do so could result in disruptions to the network.

The advantages of the delegated PoS consensus are apparent. First of all, nodes with small balances have an impact on the selection of validator nodes, which if indirect is still proportionate to its financial balance. In their combined mass, these nodes are likely to prevent major players from seizing control of and centralizing network management processes. Nodes with the best design and the highest level of trust from the network will create the blocks directly. As concerns the final factor of import, there is no need to block off large amounts of crypto funds on accounts, so that the validator can constantly prove their financial viability and thus obtain the rights to create blocks in the network.

Again, this is not to say that the concept of PoS has no potential problems. This protocol can also be subject to various attacks, theoretically among which is the now-familiar "51% Attack." However, unlike PoW systems, where it would be necessary to assume control over at least one half of the network's total computing power, with PoS, this requires control over at least half of all the cryptocoins in the project. In both concepts, however, such an attack would have a similar negative consequence in that it would entail a massive undermining of the trust placed in the network as a whole and the depreciation of the local cryptocurrency, therewith also reducing the attacker's gains to naught.

One possible complication of PoS consensus is the Nothing at Stake attack. Such a situation occurs when an unscrupulous validator tries to create and sign blocks in various branches of the chain that were formed randomly or intentionally. As concerns of PoW, this miner's behavior is irrational, since it thus distributes its computing power between branches and reduces its own chances of creating a block in any of them. On the other hand, in the PoS model, it runs no risk because it does not expend any money or computational resources to create blocks in competing branches. Meanwhile, such activities will certainly violate the consensus, as the network will not be able to reach any such consensus. All projects that employ the PoS model have attempted to confront this issue with varying degrees of effectiveness.

Another important property of PoS in its classical form is the absence of an equivalent to the miner's fee. Since there is no mining per se, it does not entail any serious infrastructure costs for its maintenance. As such, the thought is that the validator's sole reward is the transaction fee which they collect. However, this scenario gives rise to the well-known dilemma of the "chicken or the egg:" if there are no mining issues, then where does money in the system come from? Different projects looking to implement the PoS principle have addressed this issue in various ways. Some follow the example of the project that paved the way for PoS: Peercoin. As we mentioned above, Peercoin implemented a hybrid consensus model, where early blocks were created using PoW mining. Then they began to "mix" blocks created by validators via the PoS protocol. At that point, PoS blocks began to dominate the chain, and the PoW was used only to make additional issues, the volume of which steadily decreased as the total number of coins in the system increased. There are also projects that decided to do without the PoW protocol entirely and created the entire emission in the first genesis block, placing it at addresses controlled by developers. Subsequently, these coins were gradually sold to new members of the network, thus establishing a circulation of money internal to the network. In this case, projects typically used the DPoS model, which allowed them to quickly and efficiently form blocks with transactions.

Returning to the Ethereum project, it is important to keep in mind that it is in the process of transitioning from one type of consensus to another. Back in 2017, the project developers announced the upcoming changes associated with the transition from mining to PoS. In the first half of 2018, there were updates associated with the transition period. It was announced that there would be a gradual decline in mining rewards – a process dubbed the "ice age" for the Ethereum network. Rumor has it that plans exist to introduce quite strict rules for validators on the "property inventory." The common assumption is that the minimum threshold for funds to be blocked by validators will be at least 1500 ether coins, which even at the current rate, which has undergone a significant correction from its maximum, corresponds to a fiat amount of more than USD 200,000. Moreover, the validator theoretically risks losing these funds because they can be destroyed if the node is caught in a Nothing at Stake attack – i.e. in the simultaneous signing of competitive blocks in different branches of the chain. The developers will announce the final rules when the update is released wherewith the Ethereum network will switch over to a PoS consensus.

The crypto industry has responded both positively and negatively to these measures. Without any doubt, those who have made hefty investments in mining ether will not be pleased by this news. The transition to PoS will leave them out of work, unless, of course, they used a graphics card for mining. The fact is that GPUs are a universal tool for mining and can be, as necessary, repurposed for mining other cryptocurrencies. Other voices are also sounding the alarm of possible security problems during the switch to the PoS protocol. Representatives of the crypto community who believe that energy-inefficient mining is a serious obstacle to the active development of blockchain technology have expressed support for the measures taken by developers. To justify their position, they highlight the fact that mining is an extremely resource-intensive process with a negative environmental impact throughout the world and also that it has met with significant criticism from national governments.

Altcoins

Human capacity for critical analysis has always been a key driver of civilization. As a school of thought, skepticism is based on the concept of doubt in the dogmatic constructs of society at large as a rational principle. After all, it is skepticism that compels us question the idealism of those surrounding us, that spurs us on to modify and improve the scientific, cultural, and social achievements of mankind. Undoubtedly, not least because of this, some representatives of the crypto industry considered the early blockchain networks to be lacking and began to create new projects with a more progressive scope of functionality. At some point, this process seemingly began to avalanche, when the total number of crypto projects began to number in the thousands, and it became absolutely impossible to cover and analyze the entire volume of information contained therein.

The capitalization of Bitcoin (i.e. the aggregate value of all bitcoins in circulation) is comparable to that of all other existing cryptocurrencies combined. Accordingly, its authority in the blockchain industry is so great and indisputable that all cryptocurrencies that subsequently are called "altcoins" in that they are considered alternatives to Bitcoin. The first altcoins appeared only a few years after the launch of the Bitcoin network, namely in 2011. These projects aimed to overcome the inconvenient aspects that they saw as natural consequences of Bitcoin itself. At the same time, one altcoins which had recently appeared almost completely copied the operational logic of its predecessor and made minor adjustments to the parameters of the processes taking place in it. This project is called Litecoin, whose very name suggests that it is a lightweight version of Bitcoin.

The Litecoin project was developed by American programmer Charlie Lee, who for some time was even suspected of authorship of Bitcoin. However, it is difficult to surmise the logical connection between remaining incognito in one project and revealing yourself in a later project which is less popular. Nevertheless, the crypto community tossed floated such ideas – at least, until attention switched to other, more odious candidates. Whatever it was, Litecoin managed to win over its own market niche and is still among the ten altcoins with the largest capitalization. What sets this project apart from its more "massive" prototype?

The number "4" captures all the differences. This multiplier was chosen by the project author to scale the parameters of the Bitcoin network. Blocks in

Litecoin are created four times faster (i.e. an average of 150 seconds) and the limit of the final issue is set at four times the value: 84 million coins. Just like in Bitcoin, the SHA-256 hashing algorithm is used to generate the addresses, but the mining mechanism has been significantly changed. To find new blocks in the Litecoin network, the special algorithm scrypt (pronounced "ess-crypt") is used, which uses large amounts of RAM. This makes it possible to counteract mining with ASIC devices, although these devices still ultimately found their way to the market.

As for the market demand for Litecoin coins, it is at an average level. For a long time the price hovered in the range of USD 2–4 per coin, but during the time of all the hype, the price reached its historical maximum of USD 358. It later fell to about USD 80, where it currently resides, and the total capitalization of Litecoin is a little less than USD 5 billion (about 5% of the capitalization of Bitcoin). Litecoin coins are quite a popular financial tool for speculative trading, and they can often be found in the listings of many cryptocurrency exchanges and brokerage companies.

Another popular altcoin and constant contender for Ethereum's position as having the second largest capitalization is Ripple, which was developed by a company of the same name to organize currency exchange processes between financial institutions – in particular, banks. Ripple was originally conceived and created for the B2B industry (i.e. for the business environment), where all interaction is carried out exclusively between legal entities. This, however, did not prevent many private crypto traders from considering the Ripple cryptocurrency as a tool for investment and large capital placements for the purpose of booking a profit on the exchange rate differences. We will consider a few of the many ways in which the Ripple project differs from other typical blockchain networks.

Interestingly, one of the key persons involved in the emergence of Ripple was Jed McCaleb, the former creator of the file-sharing network eDonkey and the Mt. Gox exchange. In 2012, in cooperation with investor Chris Larsen, he was the one who made the proposal to Ryan Fugger, the developer of the RipplePay payment protocol, to create a special cryptocurrency that could be used in interbank currency exchange operations. However, a year later McCaleb left Ripple and founded the Stellar project – its direct competitor – which is also among the top ten cryptocurrencies in terms of capitalization. What was the main point of creating these projects?

Traditionally, cross-border bank payments involving conversion from one national currency to another have relied on expensive interbank intermediary infrastructure. Precisely the operation of this infrastructure was the reason behind the high fees that bank customers had to pay when making transfers. Occasionally, if the transfer required one third-world currency into another, the fees could be the equivalent of tens of dollars, making the transfer of smaller sums of money financially unjustified. In addition, these transfers would often take considerable amounts of time, which was also extremely inconvenient for many clients of traditional financial institutions.

The Ripple project was designed to be a fundamental solution to this situation and free bank customers from having to pay exorbitant commission fees to global financial networks acting as intermediaries in the processes of money transfers and currency conversions. Additionally, it included plans to significantly reduce the average payment time by offering the best conversion rates from one national currency to another. This required involving a large number of banks from all over the world in the project by establishing proper incentive in the form of reducing the costs of cross-border payments. Many consider Ripple to have solved this problem quite successfully by directly bundling and confirming transactions in an average of just four seconds via its distributed network of counterparties. More and more banks are joining the Ripple network, which is indicative of the project's active development.

As for the technological aspects, Ripple has one important difference from traditional blockchain networks – namely, its lack of mining. The entire volume of Ripple cryptocurrency was generated immediately at the start of the project, and the total number of coins amounted to as much as 100 billion units. By the way, this large-scale emission catapulted the cryptocurrency into the top list in terms of capitalization. Moreover, 60 billion coins are stored in a special reserve and completely withdrawn from circulation. The cryptocurrency of the project is used for direct interbank transactions, which are displayed in a common distributed register. This network uses the fee to protect against transactional spam, but since there is no mining on the network, it is simply burned, thus reducing the total number of coins in circulation. The total bandwidth of the Ripple network is about 1500 transactions per second which is quite the achievement for a similar decentralized network.

Returning to the review of popular altcoins, it would be unthinkable to not discuss one of the smart contract platforms competing with Ethereum: the EOS project. Launched in January 2018 by the company block.one, this platform lets you create smart contracts in a distributed blockchain network. These smart contracts are written in the popular programming language C++.

Unlike Ethereum, where the language Solidity was specially developed for the purpose of creating smart contracts, in the EOS platform developers can use familiar tools for writing software code. The network uses DPoS as its consensus protocol which allows transactions to be confirmed in just a quarter of a second. Nodes creating blocks are selected in a continuous voting process among the owners with the largest holdings of EOS, the local cryptocurrency. That said, a delegate node that fails to create a single block during the day is automatically released from this honorary duty in the future.

The EOS network has a curious transaction format in that it contains a hash of the previous block. This makes it possible to avoid duplication of transactions in the branches (forks) and can conclusively state in which branch an individual network user is located. The EOS network does not levy a fee for transactions, and the cryptocurrency is used in smart contracts and to support the circulation of tokens created in the system. In total, there are about 900 million EOS coins in circulation. The current capitalization of the issue is slightly less than five billion dollars, which places the project among the top five in this category. As in the Ripple project, there is no mining in the EOS network, and coins can only be obtained by purchasing them directly from the developers or via cryptocurrency exchanges. During the initial placement of EOS cryptocurrencies, over the all the phases of the ICO, the developers managed to raise about USD 185 million for the further development of the platform.

To wrap up the section on altcoins, I would like to take a look at one last project called IOTA. It was originally conceived as a way of transferring data and payments, free of commission, between devices in the so-called "internet of things." The "internet of things" concept was developed as a way of networking various devices, such as household appliances. Visionary technologists predict that the day is not far off when a person will be able to delegate the rights to financial transactions to ordinary household devices, which will be able to automatically purchase the resources necessary for them to operate in an uninterrupted fashion. In this context, the IOTA network can become a convenient environment for such transactions.

It should be highlighted that the IOTA project does not use the blockchain structure in the classical sense. In other words, the network does not have any blocks per se; instead, it only contains a set of interconnected transactions which forms so-called directed acyclic graphs. Such graphs do not have any cycles, and their edges move only in one direction. Based on this principle, in the IOTA network, each new transaction confirms two old ones, and such confirmations form a whole "web" of verifications, thus protecting the network from the problem of double spending. The network's cryptocurrency is called "iota," and its finite issue totals a staggering 2,283,277,779,530,761 coins. As there are no blocks, no mining is carried out in the network, and all transactions are free of commission. For ease of use, iota coins are counted by the million, or in MIOTA. At present, the project's capitalization amounts to about USD 900 million.

In looking at the projects of various altcoins, you can periodically encounter implementations whose names are derived from the names of popular blockchain projects. At the same time, they position themselves as fine-tuned copies of their basic prototypes that at some point took on a life of their own. These are called altcoin fork projects. How do they appear and become part of the blockchain industry?

Forks

It can happen that a group of like-minded people once brought together under the auspices of a community – creative, political, commercial, or any other – falls apart following a breakdown of the shared understanding.

Often, this takes the form of a serious divergence of views on what they are trying to create or develop together. And then the community splits and reorganizes into new groups, each of which having its own perceptions of the most effective ways to move forward. As such, each of the branches share a common history, while having their own different visions of the future. This process is natural, endless, and even commonplace because it constantly manifests itself in vastly different spheres of human life. The same is also true of the blockchain industry, as the straightforward presentation of various projects in it has proven quite conducive to such processes' naturally occurring.

Indeed, the vast majority of projects based on blockchain technology openly publish the source code of their programs, so that anyone can have access to them. They do this for several reasons. Usually, open source is a logical choice when it comes to organizing a decentralized network with equal rights for participants, where the developer themselves have no special preferences. In addition, the availability of open source code guarantees the network participants full transparency of all processes taking place in it, as well as their full compliance with the adopted consensus protocols. Finally, it allows anyone to check the code for malicious elements that could theoretically be embedded in the program at the development stage. In other words, it is necessary for developers to provide the open source code to ensure the credibility of the project in the eyes of all its participants.

However, there is a downside to this tradition of transparency. It creates highly favorable conditions for third parties to lift the source code – partially or completely. It does not matter whether the individuals in question once belonged to the development team or are from a completely third-party entity looking to improve the project by making modifications and additions to the extent that they deem efficient and beneficial. This is how core projects forms branches which the blockchain industry refers to as a "fork." We already took a look at this concept in our discussion of how branches emerge in a chain of blocks at times when different nodes simultaneously create competing blocks. However, such forks did not give rise to new projects, since the consensus protocols in blockchain networks were programmed to opt for the legitimate chain and simultaneously reject the illegitimate branches.

However, there is another kind of fork which entails a somewhat greater degree of complication, since we are talking about direct changes in the code of the client portion of the blockchain project.

There are two types of such forks – soft and hard. More often than not, the project developers themselves choose to initiate the forks in cases where some changes must be made to its logic. If said changes did necessitate replacing the node software, then it can be considered a soft fork. When activating soft forks in the network, there is no need to agree new rules with old nodes. Soft forks can take place quite frequently. In fact, they occur with the release of new versions of the client node software, which does not introduce any irreversible changes in the rules of the network or in the format of data storage.

Hard forks, however, are a different story altogether. If some nodes do not accept the new changes and update their software, they will no longer be able to interact in any way with the nodes that have agreed to these fundamental modifications. If the stubborn nodes are sufficiently numbered, they can form their own separate network, which will continue to practice the old principles adopted before the large-scale revisions of the project code. Or, on the contrary, a group of active network nodes wishing to implement changes which it views as progressive can find themselves facing off with conservative developers who refuse to integrate said changes into the code, insisting instead that it would be inadvisable to do so. Both scenarios have the same consequence – a hard fork is formed, which generates two bases of blocks instead of one. From this moment onward, each chain begins its own life in the blockchain industry.

The new project resulting from a hard fork will be run by a team of developers put together either on the basis of a previously established initiative group or at the bidding of a businessman who in some cases intentionally triggered the split. The project gets a new name – usually derived from the name of the primary project. The local cryptocurrency is also renamed and receives a separate market ticker – i.e. an abbreviated name comprised of several symbols. At this point, the project code is modified in accordance with the contentious features that catalyzed the project splitting into two branches. Generally speaking, such a process does not drastically differ from that which occurs in a normal business environment, when a team is assigned from some company and creates its own business on the basis of experience acquired (and occasionally resources borrowed) from the previous workplace.

To avoid potential confusion, any future use of the term "fork" will be in reference to a "hard fork." For now, let's consider the following question: is the occurrence of forks a negative or positive phenomenon for the core projects? As often happens, this scenario can be viewed from two perspectives. Certainly, the emergence of a competing project which strongly resembles the core project in terms of functionality, makes the user audience for both of the networks much less defined. Typically, the core project experiences a slight dip in the demand for the local cryptocurrency, and on the exchanges one can witness a decline in its volume traded. Nonetheless, there is a silver lining for holders who owned significant volumes of the core cryptocurrency prior to the two projects' splitting. The point is that at the moment of the fork being created, the block database is copied to the new branch one by one. Only at this point do the databases begin to desynchronize the lists of transactions which are now being created in each of the branches independently of each other. What does that mean?

This means that the owners of the cryptocurrency in the core project automatically receive precisely the same amount in the new network, denominated in the fork cryptocurrency. This is because up to the moment of the split, all the old transactions in both projects remain exactly the same. Therefore, if a new cryptocurrency receives some kind of market valuation, then for those who own it, this event can be regarded as an additional monetary gain, since their balances in the main network remain unchanged. They can sell the cryptocurrency obtained as a result of the fork on the exchanges and earn some additional income, thus partially compensating for the inconvenience associated with the projects' splitting. It is quite likely that the market value of the fork cryptocurrency will be significantly lower than that of the primary one, but any price above zero will already represent a net income that essentially materialized out of thin air.

The logic of creating forks is based on overcoming the fundamental limitations of their core prototypes. Within a few years following the launch of the Bitcoin network, the limits of its potential scaling began to be outlined. Consideration was given to factors related primarily to transaction processing speed and block size, which was limited to one megabyte. Historically, the first fork of Bitcoin was the implementation of BitcoinXT that took place on August 15, 2015. The key distinction in this fork from the classic Bitcoin was an increase in the block size to 8 MB, with subsequent plans to double the block size annually. At first, the fork was favorably received by the Bitcoin community, and the number of BitcoinXT nodes grew to about 4000. However, in 2016, its popularity began to decline, and the number of nodes fizzled out to a couple of dozen, which signified the actual "death" of the fork.

BitcoinXT's unenviable fate did not stop attempts to create a fork of Bitcoin designed to wrest the laurel of glory from the pioneer blockchain project. On August 1, 2017, a project was launched with ostensibly more fanfare than any other fork in the Bitcoin network – BitcoinCash. Supported by the well-known activist of the blockchain community and cryptocurrency investor Roger Ver, this fork began to gain popularity in the crypto industry. In many senses, the nature of the project is reminiscent of BitcoinXT because it also ramped up the size of blocks to 8 MB. In addition, BitcoinCash applied several other technological innovations, such as an accelerated change in network complexity and the introduction of a new type of transaction with enhanced cryptography. A year after the launch of BitcoinCash, the size of the block in its network had already become 4x larger – 32 MB.

Much attention was given to the fork due to the support of an AISC device manufacturer from China and several large mining pools. It is all too apparent that their interest was dictated by a desire to give a boost to the markets for equipment and to attract even more nodes to the mining process. Nonetheless, it should be noted that not all miners were in favor of increasing the block size, as this would potentially reduce the transactions fees to be collected. With only short-term monetary goals on their mind, miners did not particularly care about the future development of the Bitcoin project, as they were quite satisfied with the existing shortage of space in blocks with a limited size. The fact that the increase in network load automatically engendered an increase in the fees indicated by senders who want to have their transactions placed in a block as quickly as possible.

Experts of the crypto industry have estimated that Bitcoin alone has undergone about seven dozen relatively well-known forks, despite the fact that the vast majority of them has not been able to gain any significant popularity. In the beginning, the news of any new pending fork had a negative impact on the market value of bitcoin. Yet, when forks began to appear – seemingly by the bundle – this process lost its influence on the price of the underlying cryptoasset, and the value of fork coins rarely exceeded even a single US dollar. Most bitcoin forks created at that time were driven solely by a desire on the part of the creators to monetize the heightened public interest in the cryptosphere. However, they did not particularly care about the value proposition that these forks could provide the industry.

After the sharp surge of the global community's interest in cryptocurrencies at the end of 2017 and the subsequent significant price correction, the number of forks took a downturn and forks in general ceased to receive much public attention. The crypto community returned the focus of its interest to developing the core Bitcoin project, which continued to dominate the crypto industry in as uncontested a manner as before all of the modifications to it began cropping up.

Of course, forks can occur not only in Bitcoin. If you look at altcoins in general, then perhaps the most famous fork occurred in the Ethereum network shortly following its launch. In the spring of 2016, a successful ICO was conducted for a decentralized investment management project called "The DAO," which was built on the basis of the Ethereum platform. The name of the project stands for "decentralized autonomous organization." It exhibited a strong example of a new approach to organizational management through its decentralization in the blockchain environment. The project was fully supported by Vitalik Buterin, the Ethereum creator, and owing partially to this factor, a colossal 12 million ether coins were fetched during the placement of The DAO tokens. At that time, the attracted investments were estimated at about USD 165 million, whereas at present it would be close to 3 billion.

However, on June 17, the leaders of The DAO announced that about 30% of all the attracted ether coins – ca. USD 50 million – had been stolen. This news provoked a panic in the market, and ether saw its value take a tumble. With time, what had happened became clear. A vulnerability had been discovered in The DAO's smart contract code which was associated with so-called "recursive calls", whereby a program procedure made it possible to cyclically launch itself. As such, it was possible to withdraw money from The DAO's wallet, place it in specially created subsidiaries, and repeat this process an infinite number of times via multiple divisions of the parent company. The entire Ethereum community faced a serious dilemma: whether to carry out a hard fork of the entire network, thereby nullifying the attacker's transactions, or to recognize such situations as naturally occurring in a decentralized open environment and try to preempt such vulnerabilities in the future.

Most of the system users, including Buterin himself, favored the hard fork. However, there were also opponents of this decision, who considered any form of "transactional kickbacks" unfair practice. They argued that the precedent left ample leeway for future interventions, thus posing a serious threat to the independent existence of the system itself. Therefore, when the hard fork did indeed transpire despite the protests and The DAO returned the stolen funds to its investors, users who objected to this course of action formed an offshoot in which such refunds were not carried out. This fork was dubbed Ethereum Classic as a way of stressing its orthodox stance on interfering in the free operation of the network. Despite the lack of support from the creator of Ethereum and rejection by the community at large, the Ethereum Classic network managed to survive. It still exists, although the value of the fork coin has not budged since then and its price amounts to about 4% of the main network's coin.

To summarize everything that we have just considered, it should be noted that, despite the bright hopes placed by the authors of forks, such project clones have not managed to assume a place of significance in the blockchain industry. It is no exaggeration to state that the vast majority of forks disappeared among thousands of other projects built on the basis of distributed ledger technology. In the blockchain industry, new projects can arise quite quickly and in large numbers. This is certainly facilitated by the openness of the source code of earlier projects which allows developers of new blockchain startups to lift entire segments in an effort to save time and resources on the reproduction of existing modules and procedures.

Ultimately, this allows blockchain technology to develop much faster than in conditions where the project source code was not made publicly available by the developers. Perhaps, due to this technological openness in the crypto industry itself, a phenomenon of far greater significance than ordinary forks appeared, which even gave birth to a separate sector. We are talking about projects that provide increased anonymity for their users. Now let's take a look at the question that one must logically pose: why are such projects so popular in an environment where anonymity is already an integral part of the technology?

Anonymity in the blockchain

There was once a time when people making a deposit at any bank could request that their name be kept secret, and this was treated with honor and respect – particularly if the sums were large. There is no point even listing all of the reasons that a bank customer might insist on remaining incognito. Indeed, the bankers themselves did not exhibit any particular interest in the individual's motives for secrecy because they felt obliged to uphold bank secrecy and to indefinitely keep their customers' funds in safe custody in their vaults. The banking industry had a longstanding practice of offering numbered accounts, when any person could access the fund who came to the bank and told the cashier the account password. Moreover, if so desired, these funds could be withdrawn in full. Alas, those "blessed" times irrevocably became a thing of the past because at some point most national governments found themselves troubled by the issue of tax evasion.

For several decades since, all banks and other financial institutions have carried out mandatory procedures for the identification of their customers. The concept of banking secrecy has forfeited its sacred status and has rather a negative connotation in the eyes of national financial regulators. These governmental organizations exercise strict supervision over the financial industry of their countries and may accuse any credit institutions under their control of one of the "mortal" sins of the modern business world – complicity in money laundering. However, instead of concentrating on the real criminals in the global financial industry, they cast a net with tiny meshing meant to catch small organizations and individuals of moderate means, whose financial transactions might not seem completely transparent – and thus suspicious – to banks and their regulators.

This causes particularly difficulty for those who conduct financial transactions outside their country of tax residence. There is a good chance that banks can close their accounts, or at least block their access to the given funds. Furthermore, they can do this without any particular reason because the bank has no desire to risk its license which a regulator could revoke in the case of serious procedural violations. Unable to cope with the huge amounts of information coming from banks, regulators are beginning to gradually ascribe their duties of combating money laundering to the financial institutions themselves. In turn, these banks are forced to reinvest their income not in the development of core activities, but to strengthen their infrastructure for monitoring customers and their financial flows. Banks are adopting increasingly strict measures toward their customers, which, of course, does not benefit the global economy as a whole. It should thus not come as a shock that human civilization found a natural reaction in the form of blockchain projects, where the virtue of anonymity is a cornerstone of the project itself. And this value has proved to be in demand among consumers of financial services around the world.

The very model of data storage and management in the blockchain implies that network users carry out their operations via impersonal addresses having the form of hashed cryptographic keys.

Thus, it is impossible to associate any individual with their blockchain address, except in some special situations. One option is that the owner voluntarily declares ownership of the address and admits to possessing the funds contained therein. Similarly, such a conclusion can be logically deducted, as, for example, in the case of Satoshi Nakamoto. No one doubts that he was the first miner in the Bitcoin network, which means that all mining rewards for the creation of the earliest blocks of the network landed on addresses belonging to him.

Despite the fact that it is not possible to determine the physical owner of a particular address in the blockchain network, in most cases one can nonetheless track the balance of the account in question and all the cryptocurrency transfers associated with it. At some point, it turned out that far from all users of networks built on blockchain technology were satisfied with this situation. These users wished to receive an increased degree of anonymity such that it was impossible to determine either the amount of funds in the accounts of a particular member of the network or what volumes of money this person transfers between accounts. The demand for additional secrecy led to the emergence of a number of projects ready to provide it to their users by using various cryptographic algorithms which conceal the original digital signatures for the transactions.

Back in July 2012, the crypto world saw the appearance of the Bytecoin project which provided complete anonymity of transactions in the blockchain. The system was created by seven developers who used the CryptoNote protocol in their project, which provides increased secrecy. However, by the time the network was launched for widespread use, it turned out that 80% of the bytecoins had already been issued and distributed in advance between the developers themselves and parties affiliated with them. This caused new, independent users of the system to distrust the project. Taking this into account, the two developers of Bytecoin – Riccardo Spagni and Francisco Cabañas – decided to create a fork in this system to eliminate its shortcomings and improve the functionality. Despite the fact that they used a significant part of the previously created Bytecoin code, it took some time to get the system operational. Launched in April 2014, the system took the name Monero, which means "coin" in Esperanto.

The Monero project uses a PoW security protocol, although the network was initially launched without mining, which only became available a few weeks later.

The network uses the CryptoNote protocol, which employs a process of so-called "obfuscation." To achieve this goal, the method of ring signatures is used thus ensuring that an outside observer cannot determine who is the true sender or recipient of the transaction. A few years later, by the end of 2017, the RingCT algorithm was further integrated into the network code, which ensures concealment of the amounts sent. Typically, in cryptosystems such as Bitcoin, the user has only one secret and one public key. The Monero network has a "spend key" for each of the addresses, similar to a secret one, as well as an additional "view key" that it can disclose to third parties to verify its transactions.

The use of a circular electronic signature mechanism does not allow other network members to correctly identify unspent outputs for a particular address and calculate its balance. Plus, all outgoing transfers are always made to single-use addresses, which renders it definitively impossible to track the movement of funds from one physical network member to another. However, the procedure for forming a ring signature involves borrowing from the blockchain database a certain number of public keys belonging to third-party network participants. Placing this masking information in the body of the transaction causes its size to drastically expand, thereby exceeding the average transaction size in the Bitcoin network by about eight times. Of course, this information redundancy makes the system cumbersome to use, which is an obvious disadvantage.

Nevertheless, as a cryptocurrency, Monero has managed to gain popularity and is a frequent choice for making purchases in online games and online casinos. Monero is among the most popular cryptocurrencies and has a capitalization of just over USD 1 billion. Although there are no ultimate restrictions on the emission of Monero, the system has stipulated a decrease in the reward for mining once 18.4 million coins have been issued. Blocks in the Monero network are created every two minutes, which allows users to quickly confirm transactions.

Somewhat prior to the Monero project, a system appeared called DASH – Digital Cash. The system was invented and developed by Evan Duffield and launched on January 18, 2014. As with other projects that operate with Bitcoin's "hand-me-down" code, the PoW protocol is used for mining here. The difference between DASH is that miners get only 90% of the reward for mining, while the remaining 10% is allocated to financing system-related projects which have been approved by the network members. At the same time, the procedure of mining in DASH is much less energy-consuming than, for example, in the Bitcoin network.

Network management in DASH is fully decentralized. Transactions are processed with a master node infrastructure. This node can be anyone from any project participant willing to offer 1000 DASH coins as collateral, thus attesting to its good network behavior. One of the masternode's primary functions is to use the PrivateSend algorithm to obfuscate transactions via the PrivateSend algorithm. In this case, we are talking about mixing payments that take place in the number of multiple rounds determined by the party sending the funds. Each time that mixing is undertaken, a new masternode is selected which has a total number of which in excess of 5000. The payment amount is divided into parts, each of which is anonymized, and then the parts with matching values are mixed. As an incentive for their activities, masternodes receive 50% of the mining reward for the blocks found by the network.

It is also interesting to note that for mining in the DASH network, a hashing principle is used which consists of as many as 11 functions of various different algorithmic nature. It's worth repeating: this is done in order to counteract ASIC mining, although hardware manufacturers did still manage to overcome these difficulties by introducing the appropriate devices to the market. In total, the network issued a little more than eight million coins with a total capitalization of about USD 1 billion. The project is quite popular and comparable in terms of use with its direct competitor – Monero.

To conclude, I would like to speak about a project, which experts in the crypto industry consider one of the most promising in terms of full anonymization of financial transactions used in decentralized payment systems. The Zcash project, which appeared at the end of October 2016, quickly gained fame and recognition as a truly anonymous payment network. This anonymizing project gained such popularity that even the police service of the European Union (Europol) expressed concern about the extent to which this network could be implemented for various criminal purposes. What was it about Zcash – in contrast to other projects dealing with increased anonymization of payments – that caused such alarm in European law enforcement?

To create anonymity, Zcash uses the zero-knowledge protocol zk-SNARK, which is essentially a functionally enhanced version of a blind electronic signature. The network itself uses two types of addresses: a shielded "z-address" and a transparent "t-address." Moreover, transactions are possible between these types of addresses in any one of the four combinations. Depending on whether the sender's or recipient's address in the transaction is a z-address, the input or output information is encrypted, or all the information is hidden, including the transfer amount. When using "t-addresses," the information remains visible. To set up the transactions, a so-called "tuple" of keys is created, consisting of a spending key, viewing key, and a payment address. Moreover, the viewing key and the payment address are mathematically calculated from the spending key, which is essentially equivalent to a standard private key.

Thus, network users decide whether to shield or disclose information about their transactions in the blockchain. If it is hidden, it is not technologically possible to trace the origin of each individual Zcash coin. In fact, only the senders and recipients themselves know about the transactions, leaving only the timestamp of the payment creation unencrypted. In addition to the actual transfer of funds, network members can send encrypted messages to each other. The Zcash project also enables the use of multi-signatures in cases when several users have a simultaneous need to manage an account jointly. To implement this function, the user needs to set the "weight" rules for each of the signatures and the value of their minimum combined "weight" in order for the transaction to become valid for the network.

The consensus protocol in the network is based on proof-of-work with blocks being created in 150 seconds, and the issue of Zcash, as in Bitcoin, is limited to 21 million coins. As an incentive, developers have allocated up to 10% of all emissions to offer additional remuneration of miners within the first four years from when the network was launched for public use. If any of the transactions has not been included in the first 20 blocks since its placement in the mempool, it is considered overdue and thus neglected by the network. The transaction fee is fixed at the measly amount of 0.0001 coins.

In terms of capitalization, the Zcash system rounds out the top 20 highest-rated crypto projects, having issued about 6 million coins with a total value of about USD 450 million.

For the purposes of this book, that description will complete the section on the most popular and universal crypto projects, and now it is time to move on to the third part of the book dedicated to topics which are in no way less intriguing. For starters, we will talk about how the blockchain technology can be practically applied in various spheres of human life. We will touch upon important topics like the interrelations between the crypto industry and the state. A significant part of the final section will be devoted to investments in crypto projects, including trading cryptoassets in financial markets. And finally, we will conclude the book with some philosophical discussions about the prospects of blockchain technology and what changes it could introduce to our worldview in the near future.

Part III

Blockchain industry

Applications of blockchain

In the previous section of the book, we devoted a fair amount of attention to the most popular decentralized platforms built on the basis of blockchain technology. These projects are universal in nature and cannot be attributed to any particular sector of the business or social world. Best of all, they would fit the definition of financial platforms since their functions have been finetuned to this purpose. This includes digital payment systems that allow for money to be transferred quickly and anonymously via a distributed network. However, that is but one application of the blockchain technology, and its capabilities extend far beyond the limits of financial transactions alone.

In the chapter, where we considered the concept of the digital electronic signature, we cited the procedure of online voting in elections for Estonian state authorities as an example. The I-Voting system, first used in local parliamentary elections in 2007, was the first of its kind to come into use at such a high governmental level. According to statistics, approximately one-third of the total Estonian electorate used the internet and asymmetric cryptography technologies to cast their ballot. However, the possibility of using blockchain technology to hold elections in Estonia currently remains in the planning phase. Oddly enough, the first country that actually used blockchain for elections was not the most high-tech country in the world: the African country of Sierra Leone. In March 2018, blockchain technology was used to verify the votes cast in the presidential election. One would only hope that countries with greater material resources and political stability will not lag too far behind Sierra Leone's example. Leveraging the capacities of blockchain in voting procedures provides them with maximum transparency and trust, since mathematical algorithms technologically remove the possibility of human factor and all its potential, indirect impact on the election results.

Blockchain also offers a wide array of opportunities for organizing trade in the commodity and precious metals markets. This technology can render the processes for trading commodity contracts more stable and transparent. This includes, inter alia, speeding up market settlements, simplifying the attraction of financing for deals being closed, as well as streamlining the issues relating to the ownership of underlying assets. As for precious stones (e.g. diamonds), blockchain technology can have a serious impact on markets where they circulate. Industrial companies engaged in the extraction and processing of diamonds, in particular, the South African company De Beers, plan to issue special passports for each precious stone and put information about them in the blockchain. Thus, the global diamond market can become almost completely subject to decentralized control and thereby significantly restrict the possible criminal turnover of precious stones. There are also a number of projects dealing with the tokenization of ownership rights to gold bars of different weights. The gold itself is not physically moved anywhere and is located in protected centralized depositories, while specially issued stablecoins, rigidly tied to the stored gold, are traded on various cryptocurrency exchanges and are used in direct OTC transactions.

In addition, the blockchain is basically ideal for building local marketplaces with the participation of many small private players. An excellent use of such marketplaces is the sale of surplus electricity generated from renewable sources. There are many small private mini powerplants, usually powered by solar or wind power. In the event of electricity surpluses during production, they can be sold in public power grids. However, due to lacking market infrastructure, it is often difficult to find counterparties for such transactions. Moreover, it can happen that the only buyer of electricity is the owner of the network – a party with a monopoly on the local energy market. For obvious reasons, the price offered for purchase in this case does not always correspond to the market conditions, the energy company may refuse altogether to enter into such agreements. In this context, there would be great utility and prospects in developing blockchain projects to conclude direct transactions between the producers and consumers of electricity. As such, initial applications of such progressive concepts have already started operating in the energy sectors of some countries.

Blockchain can make tremendous contributions in the field of medicine. It can be used to organize decentralized storage of patients' medical data – e.g. extracts from their medical records, medical histories, prescribed medications, and other information that is typically distributed among a host of medical institutions. Under most circumstances, it is quite challenging, and often impossible, to consolidate all of this data. It goes without saying that the information in the blockchain database itself must be stored in encrypted form. At the same time, access to it – in whole or in part – may be granted only by the patient themselves at the request of the hospital or clinic offering medical services to the individual in question. In addition, the blockchain can be used to track the supply chains of drugs as a means of combating their falsification. The same applies to accounting for the production and supply of drugs containing narcotic substances as such drugs should be subject to strict control. Finally, blockchain can significantly facilitate the work of the insurance medicine industry by placing smart contracts in a distributed database to conduct automatic payments for medical services rendered. Admittedly, prior to making any payment, such smart contracts will need to verify that all the necessary conditions of the particular insurance contract have been satisfied.

The fight against counterfeiting goes far beyond the production of medicines. All industries related to the production of goods and their logistics find themselves compelled to solve such problems. In the blockchain industry, projects exist that provide services for the special labeling of goods and then subsequently place information about the place of production and the entire supply chain of goods in a distributed data ledger. Any member of the network can then request and check this information to verify the legal origin of the goods purchased. As a side note, this form of commodity marking is well protected from unauthorized reproduction, so expectations are that there will be a quite high degree of consumer confidence in such models of combating counterfeiting.

Blockchain could also offer enterprising solutions for the tourism industry. As in most industries, pricing for products in the tourism industry is heavily influenced by the mark-up of intermediaries, which in some cases account for one-third of the final cost and even more. In this case, the use of blockchain technology, which allows producers and consumers of travel services to conduct transactions directly with one another, completely eliminates the margin of the expensive intermediary from the final pricing. This includes services for purchasing tickets for various modes of transport and hotel reservations as well as the sale of by-products related to tourism – e.g. excursions. Of course, in situations with services being distributed and performed outside of the blockchain systems, such decentralization will inevitably entail situations of conflict that require resolution. And this is one of the main problems of business disintermediation, whereby the intermediary role is completely removed from the process of purchasing a product or service. That said, solutions are already in place, and we will consider them later.

Not so long ago, the world of social media found itself buffeted by scandals following leakages of users' personal data. This included several million Facebook users, whose data was in the possession of third-party companies that leveraged this data for both commercial and political purposes. Other social networks have also experienced similar difficulties. Admittedly, the cause was no mystery: the companies managing these projects failed to demonstrate a sufficiently mindful approach to storing users' personal data – not to mention the cases where data was deliberately sold to interested outside parties. Upon closer analysis, however, we see that the root of the problem lies in the fact that the data was stored in a centralized fashion. Furthermore, the incidents listed above are merely natural ramifications of such a model.

Indeed, this begs the conclusion that these issues can only be solved by decentralizing the ways in which user data is stored on social media and messengers. Also here, the blockchain technology can save the day. Implementing the distributed ledger technology will allow users to control their personal information – its publication, storage, and usage. Information stored in a decentralized manner and encrypted with strong algorithms simply cannot be wielded for illegal purposes by third parties. Of course, drawbacks in working with such systems will occur primarily because of the inability to remove information which had previously been placed there. On balance, however, the advantages will essentially outweigh the other factors related to the use of decentralized systems. Of course, it will be very difficult for projects based on blockchain technology to win over their fair market share from popular centralized social networks. Hopefully, however, they will succeed with time, since the demand for the security of personal data storage is clearly rising.

Finally, blockchain is finding widespread application in the entertainment industry – in particular, for setting up gambling and bookmaker services. It's well known that casinos and bookmaker companies draw their income from the so-called "negative expected value" for their clients, which is incorporated in the conditions of the games and betting on events. What does that mean? Any game or dispute involves, as a rule, three variants of the final outcome: win, lose, or draw. Typically, the organizer tips the payment conditions in their own favor. In other words, in the event of a winning event taking place the client receives a little less money than could be expected if reward distribution were entirely fair. Precisely this imbalance serves to provide a pseudo-guaranteed profit for the organizer given significant total volumes of gaming transactions over a long time period of time.

The party receiving the bets is a classic element of centralization and sets aside remuneration for themself. This can take various forms, some of which are more subtle – i.e. the disbalanced payment terms as described above. Blockchain technology makes it possible to remove this element altogether, thereby introducing equilibrium for both parties into the terms of gaming transactions. Even today, gambling projects exist where there is no central organizer. As such, there is no need to create conditions that place one of the parties on unequal footing. In addition, the very use of blockchain technology ensures full transparency and honesty in direct operation of the games, since the platforms have made their code open for review by any entity participating in the project.

Drawing up a list of all the industries where blockchain technology could be applied to efficient effect would be a tiresome endeavor as the list would simply wax on endlessly. Once again, the main purpose of introducing this technology is to reduce or eliminate the intermediary role and the costs associated therewith. Another factor of importance is ensuring the transparency of the rules and procedures as a way of considerably boosting consumer confidence in such systems as a whole. At the same time, in order to maintain the efficiency of such projects, there is a need to ensure the cross-border movement of capital between the worlds of cryptocurrency and fiat currency. In turn, this cannot but compel various national governments to pay close attention to the processes unfolding in the cryptosphere, so as not to lose control over tax revenues from the business environment which they regulate.

As noted earlier, government regulators express the greatest concern at the possible legalization of funds which were illegally obtained. Quite often, government officials thus find themselves compelled to take actions that clearly impede the development of advanced technologies in the modern financial world, including blockchain. Indeed, it is not difficult to note the fairly complicated relationship between the blockchain industry and the state, but some of these aspects merit more detailed consideration.

Blockchain and the state

Scientific disciplines that study the business world unequivocally state that public administration is the least effective form of management as such. The reasons abound: low managerial competence of political appointees and a clear lack (or, conversely, overabundance) of resources controlled by the governing entity. Generally speaking, the negative impact on management processes derive from poorly defined strategic goals, feeble systems of overseeing executive discipline, insufficiently defined forms of personal responsibility, and – not to mention – weak financial incentives for managers. Finally, the use of political populism as a tool to gain and retain state power in most cases undermines any economic model, even if it has already exhibited any measure of success. The nature of government is based on political ideologies – right-wing, centrist, or openly left-wing. The political strategy of the state is carried out by democratic or authoritarian methods, with systemic corruption being a proverbial bedfellow of the latter type.

As a rule, nations draw in their revenue from one of two main sources – taxes levied on entrepreneurs and the working population as well as the extraction and sale of natural resources. In this context, we will define the state as the set of bureaucratic institutions necessary for it to function. Clearly, the very existence of national management infrastructure vitally depends on taxes being paid. As such, the majority of public officials lend a great deal of attention to this matter. What methods of control does the state use? For starters, the most important systemic component of the business environment in most countries of the world is its national financial market. The system of monetary relations can have a determining impact on whether the national economy will develop actively or stagnate and inexorably end up in an economic depression.

Given the critical importance of the health of the financial industry, the state makes constant efforts to exert managerial influence over it – and regulate it. The state has at its disposal the necessary tools for such: a set of sectoral laws as well as the infrastructure of bureaucratic and law enforcement agencies. Admittedly, a high degree of regulatory rigor is more the result of the industry's particular evolution rather than a reality established from the very beginning. For quite a long period throughout the history of civilization, the financial markets of various states functioned on the basis of ordinary self-regulation. However, the global financial crises have forced public authorities to adopt stricter regulatory approaches. Several states (including democratic ones) began shifting from typically libertarian models to openly protectionist and even repressive forms of influence on the financial industries under their control.

Over the past decade, a regulatory strategy has become widespread which primarily aims to combat the laundering of money by business entities that evade legally established tax payments. The emergence of blockchain technology with its own decentralized and independent infrastructure, as well as inherent anonymity, has complicated the processes of necessary supervision over the movement of financial currents. However, not until the first projects built on the basis of blockchain technology had become relatively ubiquitous did the authorities pay any serious attention to them. Their initial lack of attention was also conditioned by the technological complexity of the concept of building payment systems based on blockchain, which presented a major obstacle to understanding the essence of the processes transpiring and the concomitant impact on the financial industry as a whole.

However, quite soon the capitalization of the cryptocurrency market reached levels of tens or even hundreds of billions of dollars. This forced several national governments to realize that the strategy of further ignoring the phenomenon called blockchain could have irreparable consequences for their state budgets. Officials faced a difficult task: how to express their stance on a new financial and technological phenomenon and then how to manage the risks associated with it for national economies? It is worth clarifying here that the severity of the measures taken by national governments in relation to the crypto industry is a direct reflection on the degree of freedom accorded for political competition in a particular jurisdiction.

In countries with a true parliamentary democracy, public officials are forced to weigh their public statements against the political impact that their words may have on the outcome of the next election. For obvious reasons, no politician would like to come across to the electorate as hopelessly old-fashioned and thus a hindrance to scientific and technological progress. Moreover, many of them are trying to play the "technology card" with their voters in an effort to boost the image of their party and present themselves as full-fledged members of the country's technological vanguard. However, being responsible for the execution of the state budget, officials remain constantly concerned about the possible loss of control over financial flows and tax revenues. Therefore, in some cases, representatives of the ruling parties or coalitions maintain public neutrality and in practice rarely support any projects related to cryptocurrencies.

In states with uncontested authoritarianism, representatives of the ruling parties have no need to compete with other political forces. Therefore, their positions are straightforward and in most cases are characterized by a set of prohibitive measures aimed at significantly restricting the use of cryptocurrency systems within a given jurisdiction. For example, a number of countries are trying to ban mining, buying, selling, and even in some cases storing cryptocurrencies. In addition, cryptocurrency exchanges and the relevant payment systems are facing scenarios where their operations are limited or completely prohibited. Yet, there is a technological complexity inherent to implementing these measures – when it is at all possible to do so – since blockchain systems are decentralized and offer anonymized use.

As such, no state can actually interfere with the activities of any of the existing decentralized blockchain networks, whether that be tracking payments within it or blocking/confiscating funds held at particular network addresses. In the classical world of fiat money, the state can always implement this set of measures with the help of banks which as centralized and licensed financial institutions are always willing to cooperate with the authorities. Nevertheless, these measures remain impossible to implement in blockchain networks. The only chance for regulators to have a marginal degree of influence on the crypto environment would be to install "border control points" between the cryptocurrency and the fiat worlds. To do this, regulators are mobilizing banks and fiat payment systems, instructing them to track the movement of capital of their customers between these financial environments of such vastly different natures.

Along with national parliaments, state executive authorities are actively creating and promoting new legislative initiatives concerning the crypto industry. Beginning in the fall of 2017, the cryptocurrency market began to boom, after which many countries began adopting laws to restrict the circulation of cryptocurrencies within national jurisdictions and then implementing them with varying degrees of rigor. The most radical examples could be seen in Bolivia and Nepal where a complete ban was placed on all activities relating to cryptocurrencies. Not much less extreme were Kyrgyzstan, Indonesia, Libya, and Algeria, where it was prohibited to purchase and sell cryptocurrencies; however, they failed to adopt a clear position on mining operations. Yet, the greatest impact on the global cryptocurrency market came from countries such as China, the US, and South Korea.

Estimates suggest that China accounts for about 70–80% of the world's mining of cryptocurrencies, thus creating a strong tie between the actions of the Chinese government toward the cryptomarket and the capitalization thereof. More precisely, this relates to the fiat equivalent price of the most popular cryptocurrencies – bitcoin, ether, and the like. In September 2017, China banned cryptocurrency trading and ICOs. Plus, orders were given for fiat and cryptocurrency funds already collected by project developers to be returned to investors. In addition, the authorities began limiting miners' ability to purchase electricity and generally obstructing their activities in an overt manner. This prompted many cryptofarmers to start moving their data centers outside of China to countries more amenable to their industry. The South Korean government also issued an order banning the attraction of investments via ICOs, and in addition a law was issued prohibiting the performance of cryptocurrency transactions from anonymous network addresses.

The United States likened the ICO-distributed tokens to securities with all the ensuing regulatory consequences, making this event a very complex and expensive process. In relation to bitcoin as a cryptocurrency, there was some regulatory conflict – a number of court precedents defined it as a conventional currency, while the US Commodity Futures Trading Commission equated bitcoin to commodities. Some individual states, such as New York and Washington, introduced mandatory licensing for companies conducting activities related to cryptocurrencies. In addition, special taxation has been introduced for transactions with this category of assets with the final rate depending on the individual state.

As concerns positive steps taken toward the legalization of the cryptocurrency market, then the undisputed leader is Japan, which became the first and so far the only country to recognize cryptocurrency as an official means of payment. Furthermore, Japan also has official licensing and regulation for cryptocurrency exchanges. Within western Europe, the Swiss canton of Zug has provided the most favorable terms for ICOs by adopting legislation in 2017 which was quite welcoming of the crypto environment. In terms of the process of creating a regulatory framework for blockchain in the European Union, the small island state of Malta has taken the lead by adopting a law on virtual financial assets in mid-2018. The legislative framework of Malta has defined the concepts associated with different types of cryptocurrencies that can be used in projects built on the basis of blockchain technology. As a result, investments flowed en masse to Maltese companies engaged in the development of blockchain projects. Estonia also chose not to remain a passive onlooker by introducing simplified licensing for cryptocurrency exchanges, which at first had more of a "declarative" than "permissive" nature. By the end of 2018, more than 500 such licenses had been issued in Estonia, after which regulators began considering possible complications of the licensing process as a way of preventing abuse by some market participants.

Despite the positive developments in the interrelations between the state and the blockchain industry, there are still many unresolved problems in this area which are hindering the establishment of a balanced regulatory policy in relation to the crypto environment. As already mentioned, one of the primary hurdles to be overcome is the anonymity of financial transactions in the blockchain. Furthermore, until project developers offer ways of deanonymizing financial flows which would be acceptable for regulators as well as provide the infrastructure necessary to identify the participants of such networks, it will be entirely pointless to discuss governmental cooperation. Regardless of the blockchain technology's renown for being cutting-edge and groundbreaking, national governments will not make haste to support its widespread implementation and use – at least not until the projects in this industry begin to meet the standard statutory requirements typically applicable to participants in the financial industry.

To hasten the day when governments begin to show favor to the blockchain industry, much work must be undertaken on the convergence of the ideological positions common to developers in crypto projects and to government officials. To this end, it would be advisable for each country to set up specialized associations with working groups for interaction with the government. Only constructive dialogue will make it possible to solve the most important task of integrating new technology into the business and social infrastructure of different states. In some countries, the crypto community is already hard at work on these issues, and in some places the first attempts are already being made.

State financial regulators have another equally important task in addition to the direct functions of monitoring the payment of taxes and combating money laundering: protecting the consumer financial market from possible abuse and outright fraud on the part of companies and individuals with a suspect reputation. Financial regulators try to advise the community, which consists mainly of non-professional investors, against rashly investing in crypto projects. Yet, what do representatives of the community think about this? What is their take on this relatively new technology on which the whole industry has sprung up?

Blockchain and society

For a long time, the study of cryptographic protocols for the purposes of creating decentralized payment systems had been relegated to a limited cohort of enthusiasts who call themselves "cypherpunks." Even when Satoshi Nakamoto's pioneering project first appeared, people who were not personally technology aficionados expressed nearly no interest in it for quite a while. The popular media hardly covered happenings in the crypto world, and interested individuals could only get their hands on moderately up-to-date information on the cryptocurrency in highly specialized professional online forums. By the end of the second year of the Bitcoin network, the number of active addresses barely numbered 1000, but a mere six months later, this figure had taken a drastic leap – by more than 20 times. At the time of the bankruptcy of Mt.Gox – a significant event in the nascent crypto industry – the number of active users totaled approximately 150,000. This figure would later undergo consistent growth, despite the fact that it did experience the occasional downward correction, particularly after periods of intense gains in prices for cryptoassets.

One would logically assume that the first generation of cryptoenthusiasts comprised representatives of the IT industry – primarily programmers. As their professional skills allowed them to grasp the principles of the new technology earlier and faster than others, they managed to fetch some degree of return on their investments at the earliest phases of existence for cryptocurrencies. Indeed, some very visionary IT specialists did not miss the chance that appeared before them and found themselves with quite a hefty profit from their investments. Those who went further in their aspirations and took part in the creation of crypto projects that ended up winning over the market's confidence became multimillionaires. As a result, it was the tales of the first crypto investors' success passing among their friends and acquaintances that most substantially contributed to raising the degree of interest in cryptocurrencies among people with no direct connection to information technologies.

After learning that the financial market has a new type of asset capable of yielding legendary returns, many made haste for the nearest cryptocurrency exchange. However, most people did not conduct even superficial research of the phenomenon in which they were going to invest their money. As a result, many hapless investors suffered losses and then hurriedly dubbed cryptocurrencies a financial bubble and even a financial pyramid. Indeed, this opinion was relayed enthusiastically by many social leaders who had even less idea about cryptocurrencies than those left with the bitter aftertaste of their unfortunate financial investments. Let's take a look at how close the critiques of cryptocurrencies as an investment instrument came to the truth.

German philosopher, sociologist, and economist Karl Marx in his work *Das Kapital* described the socioeconomic phenomenon called "capitalism," claiming that one of its significant phases is the recurring crisis of overproduction. This cyclical pattern implies a succession of periods of strong economic growth and, inevitably, a subsequent depression. Indeed, in the more than 100 years since Marx published his work, the world has been shaken several times by financial crises of varying severity, which have been followed by prolonged economic stagnation. Governments took many years to recover from the collapses and then – after initial recovery in the market – to start showing signs of economic growth.

In the run-up to the financial crisis, the national economies were, almost without exception, showing signs of overheating, which could be seen in the fact that the excessive availability of investment funds led market participants to purchase in excess instruments traded on the markets. The stock exchanges had been exhibiting exceptional levels of activity and widespread tendencies to invest in equities of companies whose true financial situation was often deplorable; yet, few investors had paid due notice to this fact. As a result, a stock bubble appeared on the market with the price of the security being in large part characterized by a speculative component. Simply put, the speculative part refers to the mark-up over the real value of the equities of a publicly traded company. When a financial crisis then occurs, overvalued stocks fall to the level of the asset value of the issuing company – and sometimes lower – as the market deals with "panic selling." One of the first investment bubbles known to the world transpired during trading of tulip bulbs at an exchange the Netherlands in 1636–1637. The excessively inflated tulip mania market eventually collapsed and led to widespread bankruptcies among late-cycle investors.

In the cryptocurrency trading market, all the same processes occur as on conventional stock exchanges, where factors related to human psychology leave an indelible mark. In turn, this means that during periods of high mass demand for investment instruments, the speculative component in their price assumes a much more dominant role than the real one. Thus, an investment bubble can occur in connection with any exchange-traded instruments, regardless of its nature, including cryptocurrencies. It is important for investors trading in financial markets of any type to determine to what extent the market is overheated and decide what risks they are willing to accept. In relation to cryptocurrencies, many analysts believe that their value is entirely dictated by the speculative aspect as they find any talk of fundamental value to be misplaced. However, we have already seen with the example of Bitcoin that some cryptocurrencies do have their own intrinsic value which is based on its cost of production.

Another classic critique of cryptoassets would liken them to a financial pyramid scheme. Let's see if that claim holds up to scrutiny. Alas, pyramid schemes are quite common in the modern world. In 1919, the very first scheme was thought up by Charles Ponzi who sold promissory notes for which he undertook to pay out USD 1,500 within three months for each USD 1,000 received. Ponzi justified such high returns with investments in postal reply coupons which he could exchange at an enticing rate. However, he did not mention that the purchased coupons could not be converted into cash, but could only be exchanged for postage stamps. Obviously, Ponzi did not purchase any stamps and focused instead solely on using this scheme to attract cash from creditors. He managed to raise about four million dollars, thereby assuming obligations amounting to about seven million obligations in return payments. The pyramid met its demise in August 1920, and Ponzi himself received a five-year sentence in an American prison for fraud.

Many countries have since seen pyramid schemes pop up that have used a variety of models for raising funds. However, all of these schemes clearly exhibit a number of common features which clearly signal that the investors are being hustled. A chief attribute of a pyramid worth noting is that the payments promised to its participants do not have any connection with the core commercial activities of the company behind the scheme. Furthermore, pyramids are – without exception – promoted by an aggressive advertising campaign accompanying the process of raising funds. Above all, however, pyramids are completely centralized endeavors with a rigid hierarchy. At the head of this structure stands the organizer as the primary ultimate beneficiary of the scheme as a whole. In the lower levels of the structures, there may work hired employees or volunteers who receive a commission for any funds raised. Initially, the organizers of the pyramid do indeed make payments to the early investors – at the expense of funds raised from later investors. However, there invariably comes a time when no further payments are made, at which point the pyramid collapses and the investors are left with nothing.

Now, let's see to what extent these characteristics of financial pyramids apply to cryptocurrencies, using Bitcoin as an example. To the decided chagrin of critics, any decentralized structure like that of Bitcoin effectively rules out the possibility of a single individual benefiting from the structure at the expense of the other investors. The Bitcoin network does not have an owner, does not conduct any commercial advertising for the sale of cryptocurrencies, and does not promise payments, except for the reward initially laid down in the competitive mining protocol for network participants. In all fairness, it should be noted that Bitcoin is a bit too idealistic an example for our purposes. In the crypto industry, there are many other projects which in theory operate in a fully decentralized manner – at least according to their developers – but in reality, this is far from the truth. In such cases, the starting issue of the cryptocurrency is created during pre-mining and placed in reserves under the oversight of the project owners for subsequent implementation. Only in such cases is it possible for the project developers to abuse their position such that the investors who have placed their funds in these cryptotokens sustain losses. There are quite a few reasons for this, but we will wait to discuss the problems of investing in ICOs in a later chapter.

Occasionally, certain individuals who have not managed to come to their own opinion of a particular phenomenon adopt by rote the views expressed by some famous individual. Throughout the ten years of the crypto industry's existence, individuals with varying degrees of expertise on the matter have expressed a whole host of views. It is worth mentioning that neutral or more moderated stances on the issue were few and far between with most of the evaluations tending to one extreme or the other – genuinely sincere enthusiasm and support or vociferous disregard replete with apocalyptic predictions. In general, business representatives tended to have more positive outlooks. Well-known economists and billionaire investors were more prone to negative outlooks on where overly optimistic investors might find themselves after purchasing cryptocurrencies. Businessmen Elon Musk and Richard Branson, as well as former head of the US Federal Reserve Ben Bernanke voiced their unequivocal support of the notion of cryptocurrencies, whereas famous investors like Warren Buffett and George Soros adopted an opposite view. Microsoft CEO Bill Gates initially spoke out in favor of cryptocurrencies, before ultimately settling on a more reserved stance.

Importantly, there exists another factor with an instrumental role in shaping public opinion about the crypto environment. Many analysts make a quite proper distinction between the concepts of "blockchain" and "cryptocurrency." Moreover, blockchain is typically received quite positively and hailed as an omen of bright times ahead. That said, cryptocurrencies meet with negative criticism accompanied by sincere wishes for a speedy extinction due to their absolute lack of utility. In this case, large commercial organization and banks serve as an important indicator. Despite their avowed rejection of cryptocurrencies, they are simultaneously developing large-scale projects to create intracorporate and even sector-wide blockchain environments with the aim of organizing the exchange and decentralized storage of information. In order to bring these projects to life, corporations even band together in large consortia with significant funding from their participants.

It is rather frustrating for representatives of the crypto community to endure negative statements the crypto industry made by varying degrees whose authority in the eyes of the cryptoenthusiasts themselves is often questionable. Generally, this leads to caustic appraisals of the technical expertise of those who took it upon themselves to predict the technological prospects of human civilization. It is difficult to state now with any certainty which of these parties will eventually prove correct in their judgments. However, there is no denying the high level of public interest in blockchain technology in general and cryptocurrencies in particular. The emergence of the cryptoenvironment has given rise to new sectors in the financial industry such as exchange trading in cryptocurrencies and raising funds via ICOs. Consequently, this process has entailed risks of an all-new nature for many consumers of financial services, which in some cases have led non-professional investors to sustain substantial losses. For this reason, we will dedicate the next section to talking about crypto trading and investments, as well as how to manage the various risks that inevitably arise.

Investment in ICOs

In 2016 – 100 million; one year later – 6 billion; and in 2018 – more than 22 billion US dollars. These numbers represent the investments in initial offerings of cryptocurrencies – i.e. in ICO projects created over the past few years on the basis of blockchain technology. In the chapter on tokenization, we briefly touched on the issue of the large-scale raising of funds in crypto projects, which in slang is sometimes called a "crowdsale." Now, we will look at this process in greater detail. Our goal is to understand what prompted so many investors to invest legitimately enormous amounts of money in the acquisition of virtual cryptoassets. Furthermore, these were often projects that had previously been unheard of and sprung up out of nowhere.

Yet, not even this kept them from taking revolutionary stakes in various business spheres and, above all, in the finance industry.

Most of the projects were conceived and proposed for implementation by groups of young IT professionals alongside representatives from the world of scientific research – usually individuals holding master's and doctoral degrees in mathematics and economics. In fact, this is how the projects were able to achieve the necessary academic gloss as these individuals put together complex mathematical and econometric devices capable of making the appropriate impression on investors. Indeed, without such an impression, there would have been great difficulty in reaching the primary aim of the initial phase: obtaining the financial backing necessary to launch the project.

Until recently, owners only needed three things to draw investments to their blockchain projects – a description of their idea, the social hype surrounding cryptocurrencies, and the lack of regulation of the crypto industry. The concept of the project was described in the form of a document called a "white paper." Usually, white papers start by identifying a certain problem, and then finishing by proposing a solution involving blockchain technology. In most cases, such documents contained sections dedicated to the release of the project's own cryptocurrency, where it indicated its cost at the initial offering. Finally, the concept descriptions were rounded out with a road map of the project stages – along with definitions – and specific timeframes for their implementation.

The project's cryptocurrencies would go on sale at the appointed time, and investors could make purchases with fiat money or another widely used cryptocurrency – usually bitcoin or ether. There were times when the volume of tokens on offer did not cover the demand existing for them as too many investors were seeking to invest their funds in the project in the hope that its capitalization would quickly grow. In such cases, there were two scenarios possible: either the tokens were given to the first buyers or the project owners took in applications from everyone and then distributed them proportionately among the investors in accordance with the volumes requested. It's clear that the buyers ended up receiving fewer tokens than they would have originally wished, but they nonetheless had the chance to purchase at least some and not find themselves entirely sidelined from the process of the initial offering of cryptoassets.

Despite the attractiveness of the ICO procedure for project developers, not all of them chose to host such events. Some developers determined that they lacked the means to conduct an initial coin offering and opted instead to distribute the coins either on the basis of mining or via retail sale to network members. In the case of a retail sale, the purchase of coins was purely utilitarian, since local tokens were required to pay the transaction fees within the system. Of course, the tokens could also be purchased for speculative purposes, but the developers did not officially position the project's cryptocurrency as a financial instrument for investment.

In the Bitcoin network created by Satoshi Nakamoto, there was no talk of an ICO whatsoever – in this enviroment, cryptocurrencies are extracted via competitive mining. In this case, the nodes that began mining coins before other network members managed to capitalize on the level of complexity of the computational problem for mining which as yet was still favorably low. Thus, the first bitcoin miners, including Nakamoto himself, managed to amass a fair amount of capital when the cryptoasset made its drastic price gains. Yet, Ethereum developer Vitalik Buterin still held his ICO, raising money for a fund that would guarantee the long-term financing for the development of his project. That said, he most definitely was not the first to carry out such a procedure.

Many consider the Mastercoin project (later renamed Omni) to be a pioneer in the field of initial offerings of cryptocurrencies. In 2013 it raised about USD 500,000 for the development of the project. By the year's end, its capitalization exceeded USD 100 million, and in 2014 Mastercoin joined the ranks of the seven largest cryptocurrencies in the industry. The project was created as an add-on to the Bitcoin network infrastructure to bolster its security and stability. Without altering the protocol of the underlying network, the project also provided for the possibility of creating cryptocurrency instruments with more complex rules of circulation than was the case with Bitcoin itself. Despite the initial interest among investors in the project's cryptocurrency immediately following its launch, quotations subsequently adopted an irrevocable downward trajectory and even the brief hype at the end of 2017 proved too short-lived to return its historical peaks. From that time on, the capitalization continued its rapid decline, hemorrhaging off nearly 99% of its value and winding up at about USD 1.5 million.

In many ways, the story of the Mastercoin project is instructive because what the developers had promised came into conflict with the functionality implemented in reality and the values that the project ultimately made available to users. Indubitably, the following competitors had their own say in the project's demise. Again, primary mention should be given to the Ethereum project, whose ICO was held in the summer of 2014 after that of Mastercoin. Just to reiterate: in just 42 days, the project drummed up an impressive USD 18 million, with one coin of ether costing, on average, about 30 US cents. At its peak in January 2018, the coin was listing at just under USD 1,400. However, like the vast majority of its cryptocurrency "siblings," ether lost more than 90% of its value from the previously achieved price peaks before closing out 2018.

After the Ethereum ICO, coin offerings became commonplace, with the golden era for public offerings of cryptocurrencies taking place in 2017 when the market witnessed a veritable avalanche of coin offerings. It was at this time that people began speaking of the "cryptocurrency hype." Despite only having the foggiest notions concerning blockchain technology, non-professional investors came in droves and confidently invested their money in various crypto projects. However, many projects existed only in the form of a general description of ideas set out in the accompanying "white paper."

In some cases, project developers had promised to implement some functionality without possessing at that time (or, for that matter, even later) the requisite technological solutions. However, the courageous crypto investors had no air of bother about them – they actively bought up all the tokens, one after the other, hoping that they would soon see at least a tenfold increase in value. In the slang of the crypto community, these investment expectations are called "to the moon." Another factor which pushed many crypto investors to make purchases was the "FOMO syndrome" – i.e. "fear of missing out." Many feared that they would miss the chance to invest their funds in the actively growing crypto industry and be relegated to the role of passive onlookers while others booked record-breaking profits.

Indeed, the value of many cryptoassets grew by leaps and bounds. The growth drivers were the main cryptocurrencies – bitcoin and ether – and the remaining tokens were quoted in relation to one of these two coins. Thus, as these two flagship cryptocurrencies made gains in relation to fiat money, they pulled the other cryptoassets along with them. Furthermore, only in isolated cases did one of the currencies post gains in relation to bitcoin or ether. "White paper" projects promised to release the first versions of the products in no earlier than one year, so investors were compelled to take the developers at their word. Business analysts repeatedly attempted to draw the attention of investors to the clear imbalance in the valuation of capitalization of crypto projects in comparison with classic startups. Yet, the investors largely failed to appreciate these warnings, which brought about a sober reckoning some time later.

First, the large-scale ICOs drew the attention of various national governments and financial regulators. Declaring one of their functions to be protecting investors' interests, these institutions began to hastily introduce measures to restrict and supervise the collection of investment funds by crypto developers, and all this took place in a way reminiscent of a financial "Wild West." First, the United States, one of the strictest jurisdictions worldwide in terms of financial regulation and oversight, flatly banned investments in ICOs. Then, China implemented similar measures, but in much stricter form – the authorities not only prohibited all ICOs, but also ordered developers to return previously raised funds to investors in full. Although many other states followed the example of the US and China, the bans imposed in these two countries had the most negative impact on financial flows in the crypto industry.

Of course, it would be incorrect to consider that the collapse of cryptocurrency quotations following the period of unrestrained growth was caused solely by environmental factors – in particular, regulatory measures. The laws dictating the financial world are such that no single energetic correction to the value of any asset made for purely emotional reasons – i.e. for no obvious fundamental reasons – can last for too long. Sooner or later, the classical principles of monetary valuation will be applied to any traded instruments, including products of the cutting-edge technologies.

In situations where the projects issuing these assets cannot demonstrate to their investors a reasonable business strategy, proper market focus, and real coverage of the consumer market, then it is only a matter of time before their capitalization falls.

As for future ICOs, this phenomenon will undoubtedly evolve further by incorporating the experience previously acquired in the industry. The changes will also entail regulatory aspects, among which chiefly figures the issue of giving investors the legal rights to own the purchased cryptoassets. At the moment, there are very few countries in the world whose laws attribute a legally similar degree of recognition to ICO-related investments as to the classical purchase and sale of units or shares in ordinary companies. In most cases, even when they are granted investment status, tokens purchased on ICOs or exchanges do not impart investors with any legal right to a proportional share of ownership in the issuing company. This means that token ownership does not grant any rights in the legal entity managing the project – neither when casting votes on strategically important issues, nor when distributing dividends, nor when selling the company to new investors. Moreover, many project developers prefer to distribute utility – rather than security – tokens, which obviously presents potential purchasers with a degree of confusion concerning their right to own a share of the project in which they are going to invest their funds.

Equally apparent is the fact that attempts to raise funds via ICOs solely on the basis of a white paper placed on the project website as a PDF will undoubtedly become a thing of the past. Before raising funds, project owners will have to attend to the necessary legal procedures: registration of the company, obtaining of any licenses necessary, as well as preparation of a prospectus to be approved by the local financial regulator. But more importantly, by the time of the ICO, the project should already have a so-called "minimum viable product" (MVP) which represents the initial stage of the project. This is necessary in order to demonstrate to investors not only the seriousness of the developer's intentions, but also the operational capability of the technological concept at the heart of the project.

As one might expect, the numerous ICOs gave rise to a nearly inordinate number of cryptocurrencies – both utility and security. It is no stretch to say that both the project developers and the newfound investors needed to make payment for the cryptoassets, whether in another cryptocurrency or in fiat currency. This could not be done without electronic trading platforms, which facilitated prompt and simple conclusion of transactions based on prices quite close to the market average. In this way, an infrastructure of cryptocurrency exchanges rose up which were built on various technological solutions and marked by a variety of instruments offered for trading. The next chapter will concentrate on this important element of the crypto industry.

Cryptocurrency exchanges

In 1406, human civilization had its first encounter with the concept of an "exchange," when the city of Bruges, now part of Belgium and in those days part of the Duchy of Burgundy, organized the first platform for exchange trading. It was founded by members of the Van der Buerse family of financiers, whose name in Latin means "purse" – hence the name for trading platforms, which would later be called "exchanges." Initially, primarily commodities were traded, but exchange trading later began to include all sorts of securities. In 1730, the first exchange appeared in Japan for the rice trade, but it was not until 1792 that an organized trading platform was established in the United States – in New York.

By the beginning of the 20th century, exchanges were widespread and operated in almost all developed countries. From the moment that exchanges appeared and nearly until the end of the last century, this is where trading took place with the help of stockbrokers who concluded transactions with counterparties by calling them out loud. The brokers' shouts indicated the name of the traded instrument, its price, and the type of the transaction (buy or sell) and served as the "exchange orders" – i.e. orders for transactions placed by parties whom the customers have authorized for such. Special bells at the exchange were rung to mark the beginning and end of trading, and to this day some exchanges continue this practice as a tribute to the traditions of time past.

With the development of the internet and information technologies, the noisy crowd of stockbrokers from the trading floors gradually started being displaced from the trading floors. Nowadays, transactions on modern stock exchanges are concluded via computer systems which have been specially designed for this purpose. In this way, counterparties to transactions can be brought together much more quickly and efficiently, and these technologies have also streamlined the keeping of records on the entire volume of trades conducted by exchange participants. The connection of stock exchanges to the internet has significantly expanded the number of traders participating in trading – now, there are not only large market participants, but also traders operating relatively small volumes of financial instruments. Nevertheless, the process of public listing remains a complex and expensive process, especially for small and medium-sized companies which lack a high level of revenue.

How are exchanges set up? In a nutshell, this can be explained as follows. Trading participants send their offers on trades to the exchange system: what instrument and at what price they would like to buy or sell. Then the entire volume of these orders is analyzed by the exchange's software, which is tasked with finding a direct comparison of corresponding orders to thus put together a deal. For example, a certain exchange trader is looking to sell 100 ounces of gold at a price of USD 1300/oz., and another person is looking to buy a certain amount of gold at the same price. When such orders simultaneously exist, the exchange matches them – i.e. registers the fact that the given trading orders align with one another. After that, the transaction is concluded with one trader giving the gold and taking the money and the other trader receiving this gold and making the payment specified in the order.

Obviously, the number of orders left unfilled always drastically outweighs the number of completed transactions; therefore, the exchange constantly displays sets of orders of supply and demand for each separately traded instrument. Orders are sorted from best price to worst price, and the top of the list features the two orders that represent the most similar values for supply and demand. The price difference between them is the concept of "exchange spread," which refers to minimum quote gap hindering the conclusion of the transaction. It is reasonably believed that the pricing of exchange-traded assets is the most fair and as close as possible to the current market values when spontaneously generated during the trading process. Of course, this statement will be true only if the exchange has a sufficiently large number of participants trading in volumes which are significant for the given instrument – i.e. only when the instrument has highly liquid.

As such, when the phenomenon of cryptocurrency burst onto the global scene, its owners immediately sensed a need for electronic trading platforms to exchange these new types of instruments first for fiat currency and then for other cryptoassets. In the section devoted to bitcoin as an investment, the first cryptoexchanges were described which have shut down their operations for now. Significant losses of cryptocurrencies due to either hacker attack or internal abuses brought about the bankruptcy of the first and most popular exchange Mt. Gox. However, subsequently, new trading crypto-platforms began to appear with greater resistance to external and internal factors. Many of them have managed to develop their activities to a truly global scale and operate with daily trading volumes in the billions of dollars.

Of course, the total volume of trading on all exchanges of the crypto industry still has a long way to go before it catches up with the classic exchanges. Even at the peak of its popularity in December 2017, the total trading volume on cryptoexchanges amounted to approximately USD 50 billion per day, while the average daily volume on the new York stock exchange (NYSE) totals about USD 1.5 trillion. Not far behind that is the NASDAQ exchange with an average daily volume of USD 1.3 trillion. By spring 2019, the daily volumes of cryptocurrency being traded had fallen to USD 30 billion. However, it's worth emphasizing that the cryptocurrency industry is still in its infancy. As such, it is still experiencing considerable price fluctuations and significant regulatory pressure, which is not the case for its more classic counterparts.

The emergence of thousands of new crypto projects led to large-scale emissions of various cryptocurrencies with their owners seeking to obtain a monetary exchange valuation for them. To do this, project developers had to make arrangements with at least one relatively popular exchange to make their tokens available for trading. During the cryptocurrency hype, this was not a simple task – more at, not a cheap task. To integrate each new cryptocurrency entailed a whole set of necessary procedures related to modifying the software of exchange trading platforms.

Security issues also played an important role because any vulnerabilities in the code of the project issuing new tokens would be automatically "inherited" by the exchange itself, which was tasked with storing a significant number of traded cryptoassets in its depositories. In the event of a successful hacker attack, exchanges risked losing a significant portion of these tokens and would be forced to compensate traders from its own capital reserves. In the first half of 2018 alone, theft from cryptoexchanges amounted to USD 761 million, and the amount of theft performed throughout the entire existence of the crypto industry is in the billions of dollars. Not only for this reason, the "entrance ticket" for those wishing to place their tokens on especially popular cryptoexchanges could easily cost millions of dollars. Additionally, it was also possible that with time some of these tokens would be delisted (excluded from the exchange trading list). This most often happened due to these instruments' having low trading volumes, which simply makes it inefficient or even unprofitable to maintain them in the exchange systems.

Most models for constructing cryptocurrency exchanges are based on the principles of centralization in the form of a classical client/server architecture. In other words, in order to trade with their assets, a trader must connect to the exchange server and send them (both fiat and cryptocurrency) to the exchange depository. From that moment, they surrender control over their funds for trading and entrusts the exchange with all issues related to the safety of their storage. They need to trust the exchanges, at least until they decide to have their funds returned to their cryptocurrency wallets or bank accounts.

History has witnessed many instances of traders unwittingly parting ways for good with their assets – in whole or in part. Many things have been at fault for such, ranging from hacker attacks to bad faith on the part of employees or owners of the exchange platforms. Similarly, centralized cryptoexchanges have always been and always will be vulnerable to repressive actions by law enforcement agencies or regulatory authorities in the jurisdictions where they are registered. The aggregate effect of these factors was that exchanges began to appear which had been built on an entirely different principle.

It's worth bearing in mind that cryptoassets by their very nature are based on decentralized principles. As such, it would be quite logical to build exchange systems on the basis of a distributed architecture, whereby a trader would not need to give control of their assets to the party organizing the exchange trading – i.e. to third parties. The question of what advantages and disadvantages are inherent to a decentralized principle of construction of the exchange platform is another matter altogether. Of course, a centralized exchange will offer much faster and more reliable operation in terms of matching and confirming the orders, since all trading orders are centrally located and available for analysis by the algorithms of the exchange platform.

Naturally, decentralized exchanges do not have servers. Each trader operates a personal client platform, which exchanges information with other similar terminals through direct connections on the peer-to-peer principle. Then, where is the database of orders stored, how are they matched, how are transactions carried out, and how do the assets traded between the counterparties physically move?

Without going into the minutiae of decentralized exchange mechanisms, generally speaking, all orders sent to the system are replicated between all of its participants. At the same time, nodes of the exchange network independently perform order matching, offering other participants options for comparing transactions so that the network can choose the best of them according to the accepted evaluation parameters and thus come to a general consensus. Sometimes the network can be divided into "federations" with either an elected or a specially appointed node at their head. These subjects of the system are responsible both for the dissemination of information and for the matching of orders in their segment, for which they are entitled to a fee. However, in this case, the information remains within the limits of their federation, thereby somewhat limiting the liquidity of the traded instruments, but significantly accelerating the overall operation of the exchange.

An obvious advantage of decentralized exchanges is the lack of a centralized governing entity capable of controlling the trading process, interfering with it, or attempting to manipulate the prices. For hackers, decentralization creates insurmountable obstacles for gaining unauthorized access to the shared asset repository, since there simply is no such thing. All assets are stored on the computers of the network participants under their own control, and the participants themselves remain anonymous, since in such an environment no identification is performed. In fact, there is no one and nowhere to do such.

Finally, such exchanges are virtually immune to regulatory pressure as their work simply cannot be stopped by any administrative order and traders' accounts cannot be frozen or confiscated. Theoretically speaking, a few nodes of the exchange network could be shut down, but it is extremely difficult to disable the entire network. However, even decentralized exchanges need minimal management, if only to develop and update the general rules of trading, as well as to maintain a listing of the instruments traded. As a rule, these tasks are implemented via elected committees; however, the manner in which they are set up occasionally lacks transparency, and in some cases the result is the emergence of a governing body, almost entirely affiliated with the structure of the developers of the exchange system. As you might guess, this approach actually centralizes the exchange's operation, thus tarnishing the very notion of creating a trading system based on a distributed architecture.

For this reason, decentralized exchanges have not yet received proper distribution due to a number of design-related difficulties – in particular, technological imperfections in the exchange of assets from different blockchain networks that are mutually incompatible. The fact is that in blockchain environments all transactions are irrevocable, and it is very important to synchronize the actions of both parties so that upon receipt of the assets, none of the counterparties could prove negligent in fulfilling their part of the obligations. Since distributed systems do not rely on the counterparties' goodwill, it is necessary either to introduce intermediary elements – such as escrow services – or to invent other ways to guarantee the performance of transaction obligations.

To solve this problem, a concept was developed called "atomic swaps." In Greek, the word "atom" is "indivisible," although scientists refuted this fact about actual atoms long ago. Nevertheless, the term has taken hold and is even used in blockchain technology to show that there must be a guarantee that the obligations in a decentralized transaction will be fulfilled by both parties without the need for trust between them. The operating principle of the atomic swap stipulates that the transaction will either be performed in full by both counterparties, or will be nullified without financial damage being incurred by any of those party to the exchange of assets. The direct technological application of atomic swaps depends on the blockchain environments in or between which the transactions are conducted.

The first atomic swap was implemented on September 20, 2017 between the Decred and Litecoin blockchains. Without going into details, we will only note that such transactions required that additional infrastructure superstructures be built on top of the main networks, which indisputably complicated the exchange processes. Since then, many teams of blockchain technologists have been working on improving the concept of atomic swaps in order to give exchanges with a distributed architecture significant advantages over their centralized competitors in the near future.

Coming back to the original reason that cryptocurrency exchanges were created, we should highlight two main categories of people using this service. The first is position investors who purchase cryptocurrencies as a long-term holding in order to extract significant income from their growth. The second is speculative traders who invest on a short-term or medium-term basis to try to extract income from both the rise and fall in the value of certain cryptoassets. In order to understand the principles and approaches of speculative trading, it is necessary to consider the financial analysis of price movements of cryptocurrency instruments.

Analysis of the cryptocurrency market

Throughout financial history – from the creation of the first trading platforms to the present day – stock traders have always sought ways of predicting the price movements of traded assets. From the middle ages to the early twentieth century, a wide range of techniques were used for this purpose, ranging from astrological and religious practices to the application of approaches that can even be considered nearly scientific. Of course, the dominant role in making investment decisions was played by insider information, whether obtained by fair means or by foul. The speed with which public information was received also played an important role – e.g. after the battle of Waterloo in June 1815, the financial house of Rothschild was the first to receive news of the British army's victory over the troops of Emperor Napoleon. This allowed the Rothschild bank first to slash the prices of UK government bonds and then during the same trading day to buy them at a significantly lower price.

However, such cases were the exception rather than the rule, so normal trading practice began to include attempts to collect and process information related to the issuers of certain securities to make informed decisions relating to the acquisition or sale thereof. Ultimately, these processes evolved into various models of price forecasting, which together formed the concept of financial market analysis. In the modern financial world, two main types of market analysis are widely used: fundamental and technical. The first method is a type of forecasting method based on the financial analysis of production and trading performance of companies issuing securities. If we are talking, for example, about national currencies, then consideration is given to the macroeconomic indicators of the countries that issue the given currency. Other important indicators of fundamental analysis include significant news related to the issuer of a financial instrument – whether it is a company or a government. The second method of analysis has a purely psychological basis and is based on the analysis of price charts for traded instruments as well as the application of various mathematical algorithms to these charts in order to identify patterns of price movement. Let's look at both types of analysis.

Fundamental analysis arose largely in connection with an event that occurred a little less than 100 years ago – in 1934 – when two American economists Benjamin Graham and David Dodd published their book *Security Analysis*. The authors aimed to provide a systematic approach to the analysis of securities in order to determine their real value relative to the current market value. As a result of such analysis, it became possible to identify either undervaluation or obvious overvaluation of the securities in question, in order to then make an appropriate trading decision. Subsequently, the principles of fundamental analysis have been actively developed, significantly expanding the range of analyzed factors that in varying degrees affect the price movements on the market.

At some point, the list of these factors grew so large that those critical of such analytical methods started talking about the impossibility of taking into account every single event that affects the price, since most of them are difficult to predict, if not entirely random.

To take a typical example, fundamental analysis is often applied to forecast the movements of national currencies; this is achieved by considering such macroeconomic parameters as inflation, unemployment, or the key rates of central banks. As a rule, a change in one of these indicators will be reflected in significant price changes in the national currency – i.e. favorable figures will portend a strengthening of the currency and vice-versa. As markets feed off of rumors and assumptions, they often manage to make the corresponding movement in full before the fundamental news is released, in which case they can even experience a reverse correction if the expectation effect surrounding the event proves to be somewhat excessive.

In contrast to its fundamental cohort, technical analysis is based on events that have already occurred – i.e. on historical quotes used to compile price movement charts for different time periods. Later, by examining such charts, technical financial analysts aim to identify price patterns or relatively stable regularities in the price movement of the traded asset. Such predictions are predicated on the assumption that trading psychology has a an approximately uniform impact on all market participants, since most of them are guided by the same methods of technical analysis.

Despite the fact that technical analysis relies heavily a chart of price quotations, which requires intensive, routine manual labor to put together (if computers aren't used), this type of analysis predates fundamental analysis by a few hundred years. It originated in Japan in the 18th century after the creation of the Tokyo commodity exchange for rice trade. Around 1750, traders began to mark price movements with special drawings, which were later called "Japanese candlesticks." This candle is a graphical construct that displays the most important price levels over a certain time interval – more specifically, the price at the beginning and end of the period, as well as the local high and low prices within a given time period. In addition, if the candle reflects an uptrend, the body of the candle is left uncolored, whereas for a downtrend, it is colored.

Japanese candlestick

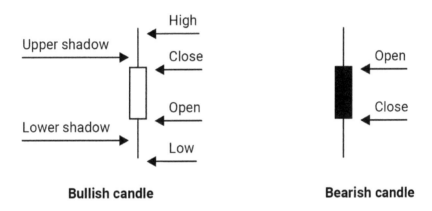

Bullish candle   **Bearish candle**

Japanese rice traders began to create similar candles at the end of each trading day, and once they had amassed a sufficient amount of data, they began to look for patterns in the price movement depending on the combination of the resulting candle figures. Combinations began to get their unique names, and then they began to be interpreted in a certain way to predict market movements. This interpretative labor later resulted in the compilation of weighty manuscripts describing various combinations of candle figures and associated forecasts of price trends.

With the advent and development of computer technology, technical analysis experienced a rebirth, whereupon charting could be entrusted to computers, significantly expanding both the time periods under consideration and the number of possible graphical elements for analysis. Using first alphanumeric and then graphical displays, analysts began to apply mathematical algorithms with various technical indicators to arrays of historical quotes.

Thanks to the analysis of price charts over a comparatively wide time range, it became possible to identify the trends in the price movement. The combinatorics of graphically displayed price changes brought the ancient Japanese graphical analysis of figures to bear again – only with a modern angle of interpretation. Technical analytics began to see terms flashing about like "head and shoulders," "double and triple tops," "triangles," and "diamonds" designating graphic figures of continuation or change of trend movements.

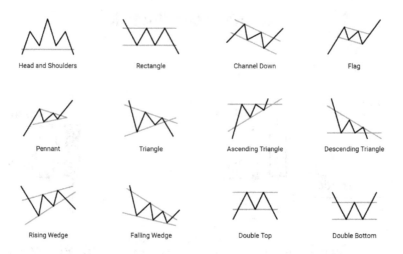

Of course, technical analysis also had its critics, who rightly believed that studying price history has little predictive weight for the future price. The point was also made that fundamental news of any practical significance will inevitably destroy all technical forecasts made previously on the basis of historicity – hence, the reactivity of the processes displayed on the price charts. Nevertheless, both fundamental and technical analyses have a huge number of followers who in most cases simultaneously employ both analytical directions in the belief that one always complements the other. On a daily basis in the financial world, there are many analytical articles and forecasts for all financial instruments quoted on the markets.

Cryptocurrencies are no exception. Yet, let's consider what types of analysis can be applied to this type of financial asset and the reasons for such. To begin with, the vast majority of fundamental analysis is not suitable for cryptocurrencies due to the lack of a centralized issuer and, thus, the impossibility of performing any related economic analysis. This primarily applies to cryptocurrencies built on decentralized competitive mining, such as bitcoin, ether, and the like. This means that no sovereign macroeconomic indicators of various states or their associations (for example, the EU) can have a direct impact on the value of decentralized cryptoassets. In fairness, it should be acknowledged that there will still be an indirect impact on the value of cryptocurrencies, but only in terms of the impact of the macroeconomic indicator on the fiat currency to which the cryptoasset is directly traded. However, at present this influence is negligible, and in analysis of the price movement of cryptocurrencies, it can be quite calmly disregarded.

Nevertheless, fundamental news for cryptocurrencies exists and can have a tremendous bearing on their value. That said, in most cases such news has a one-time effect, as it often associated with the decisions of national governments to restrict or ban the circulation of cryptocurrencies. Moreover, there exists a handful of countries where news can have a strong effect on cryptocurrency quotes. Above all, this list includes China, the United States, South Korea, and Japan – i.e. the countries where the largest volumes of cryptocurrency trading on the relevant exchanges are concentrated.

If the cryptoasset is issued centrally and, importantly, is not a utility token, but rather a security token, then the fundamental analysis is partly applicable to the evaluation of the managing company issuing the security. In such instances, classical assessment can hardly be used due to the fact that the majority of management companies are newly launched startups, which have typically not yet managed to make any profit from the project. Therefore, the analysis should cue in on typical startup parameters like the experience of the project development team members, the proposed implementation strategy, the relevance of the product and its market positioning, the amount of investments raised, the availability of an MVP, etc.

As concerns cryptocurrencies, technical analysis seems to be the more effective option given its close connection to the psychology of market participants. This means that the behavioral patterns of crypto traders are not much different from those that we are used to seeing in the classical markets. Many technical analysts recognize the workability of various indicators – primarily graphical ones including both trend lines and special figures that signal various trends. The psychological influence on price should also not be underestimated as strong preference is given to "aesthetic" values – i.e. 1, 10, 100, 1000, etc.

As already noted, technical analysis came before fundamental analysis, since its principles are based on easily collected data on trades at specific sites and points backward in time. With the streamlining in how information on issuers or indicators of national microeconomies is gathered and circulated, fundamental analysis comes to the aid of technical analysis. In these aspects, cryptocurrencies are largely following the path already trodden by fiat traded instruments.

To wrap up this section, I would like to say a few words about the trading strategies employed by traders in the cryptocurrency markets. Just as with classical financial markets, we can distinguish two overall strategic approaches – speculative and position. Speculative trading is short-term and ranges from intraday trading where positions are opened and closed by a trader within a single day to holding positions for several days, but not more than one week. Such a strategy presumes a fairly high degree of volatility in the cryptocurrency being traded – i.e. high amplitudes of possible quotation fluctuations – and you can make a profit by correctly "catching" the desired overshot in price.

Position investment is described by the principle of buy and hold. In the hope of a considerable price gain, position traders can hold their investments for months or even years. However, it also happens over the time that the position is held, a traded cryptoasset can reach both historical peaks and unprecedented lows in its value. In cryptocurrency slang, long-term investors are called "hodlers" which was distorted from the word "holders." This word was introduced into the crypto world in December 2013 by a user from the popular Bitcointalk forum. Being intoxicated (as the author of the meme later admitted), they made a mistake and wrote "I am hodling", and this phrase was picked up by other participants of the forum. This term later came into widespread use to describe the behavior of conservative investors who expect a long-term upward price trend.

To wrap up the section on investments in cryptocurrencies, it is perhaps pertinent to call attention to one important problem faced by many investors, especially those who can be described by the word "hodlers." More specifically, we are talking about holding cryptocurrencies purchased for the long term in the relatively unstable environment where cryptoassets circulate. A number of factors can be mentioned here, including technological vulnerabilities in the code of cryptowallets, hacker attacks, and bankruptcies of cryptoexchanges. Insufficient attention to security and risk management can bring about a horrendous consequences for the investor. In the next chapter, we will address the issue of managing these risks.

Custody of cryptoassets

In the section devoted to bitcoin as an investment, we read about a Norwegian student who for testing purposes made a purely symbolic purchase of bitcoins while working on a university thesis paper. Several years later he recalled this experiment from his university days only to discover that the price of his existing cryptoassets had skyrocketed. Restoring access to his bitcoin wallet was a somewhat time-consuming endeavor. Thankfully, this story too had a happy ending as the former student did manage to recover the password to his wallet, and he was able to assume active control of his unexpectedly found wealth.

However, not all stories ended so well as there are a variety of ways that owners of cryptocoins often lose the private keys to their wallets. In most instances, this involves – plain and simple – a failure of computer equipment, especially hard drives, where the precious data was stored. As the young crypto community found it particularly urgent to come up with a solution to the problem of safely storing digital coins, the industry was not slow to respond to the public demand. As such, various projects began to be systematically released which made it possible with varying degrees of success to solve the problem of holding cryptoassets – whose value continued to climb by the day – in a satisfactorily reliable manner. Let's take a look at the variety of methods of storing cryptocurrencies currently available to users today.

Like conventional fiat money, cryptocurrencies are stored in special wallets. Generally speaking, crypto wallets are broken down into one of two types – "hot" and "cold" wallets. Hot wallets are either physically located on user devices with an internet connection, or they are centralized internet services which can also include cryptoexchanges. Cryptocurrency funds stored in hot wallets are available at any time for transactions – i.e. for spending. Cold wallets do not have a permanent connection with the digital world and are somewhat similar to a safe. Before one can spend cryptoassets held in a cold wallet, a number of procedures must be conducted in order to extract them from storage.

Hot wallets can be further broken down into ones that their users control independently, and one where management and control functions are delegated to third parties – i.e. centralized services. As it is known, the rights to possess crypto funds are granted by controlling the corresponding private keys to the associated accounts. Therefore, each user decides for themselves whether to accept the trouble and risk of keeping their own private keys and ensuring the safety of their storage or to entrust these duties to one of the popular internet services that provide wallets for various cryptocurrencies. In the first scenario, the user must become a node of the corresponding blockchain system, which will requiring downloading – fully or, at least, partially – to their device the block database associated with their crypto funds. Typically, this requires allocating a fair amount of space on local storage devices and constantly updating the block database, which can take some time.

The vulnerabilities entailed in this method of storing crypto funds owe to the fact that given its connection to the internet, the user's device is susceptible to being attacked by hackers looking to steal private keys. In addition, various computer viruses (i.e. "Trojan horses") can place a special code on the user's computer to search for private keys from various blockchain environments and send them to the developer of the virus. Possessing the private key from the blockchain address grants full control over the cryptocoins located at the given address. In light of the wide array of security threats that one might experience in independently maintaining the private key infrastr ucture, many technically inexperienced users entrust professionals with their crypto savings. Indeed, there are services that offer centralized solutions for storing various cryptocurrencies.

Not having complete control over their own crypto funds could undoubtedly cause owners to worry about the safety of their holdings. It should go without saying that all the mainstream projects offering centralized storage of cryptocurrencies pay quite a bit of attention to protection against hacking and have a staff of specialists with qualifications in computer security. Nevertheless, such services are exposed to a much greater risk of being targeted by a hacker attack than is the case for private owners of cryptocurrencies. In addition to the technological threats, there are also risks of another nature – potential abuse by the owners or employees of project management companies. The story of the bitcoins that disappeared from the Mt. Gox exchange remains fresh in the memory of many, and this is not the only instance when users of a centralized service lost their cryptoassets for one reason or another.

Above all, users of centralized storage services for cryptocurrencies should adopt a balanced approach to choosing the site itself. Attention should be given to factors like the company's age, its history, and reputation as well as whether its security system has ever been hacked and/or cryptoassets stolen. Similarly, one should attribute proper weight to the jurisdiction where the company is registered and whether it possesses a license as this at least signifies that the company's activities are under regulatory supervision, which means regularly undergoing various kinds of audits – financial and technological. Given all the potential risks, one can quite satisfactorily select a suitable form of using hot wallets to store crypto funds, but if the user has higher security wishes, it makes sense to focus exclusively on cold wallets. What are the advantages and disadvantages of storing cryptocurrency in this way?

Cold storage can be implemented on any computer device which does not have an internet connection. Hardware solutions resembling conventional flash memory devices have become quite popular. As a matter of fact, such hardware wallets are essentially glorified flash drives with the sole difference being that they contain special software for storing cryptocurrencies. Often, these devices are equipped with a small LCD screen that displays a variety of useful information – such as the balance of the cryptocurrency wallet – when connected to a computer.

Devices are only connected to computers when making a transaction, so stealing their private key is no easy matter. In addition, some devices also contain a special button to generate an electronic signature of transactions which must be physically pressed when making a transfer, thus rendering the theft of classified information nearly impossible. The most popular models of hardware crypto wallets are currently, Trezor, Ledger Nano S, and KeepKey. All of these models carry a somewhat hefty price tag, but they do indeed provide a sufficiently high level of security for storing cryptocurrencies. Admittedly important in its own right, such security takes on all-new relevance when it comes to the storing amounts with a considerable fiat equivalent.

For the largest private or institutional owners of cryptocurrency reserves, there are even special underground bunkers, which in terms of security differ very little from the most serious bank vaults. There are companies worldwide that provide quite expensive, but extremely reliable service for storing large amounts of digital assets. Massive steel doors, bulletproof glass, barriers against electromagnetic interference, exceptionally rigid identification requirements for visitors – this is but an excerpt of the attributes of places where cryptoassets worth billions of dollars are stored in the form of their owners' private keys. Despite the fact that such structures are constantly targeted by cybercriminals, no one has ever managed to overcome all the cascades of protection to seize possession of at least one of the secret keys stored there.

To round out the description of the types of cold storage of cryptocurrencies, another very simple, yet quite secure method deserves a mention. Oddly enough, we are talking about wallets in common paper form. After all, if owning a cryptocurrency account is based solely on controlling the private key associated with it, then why can't it just be printed out on paper and stored in a safe or even a safety deposit box? On the internet, one can find many services that allow you to turn any blockchain account into a printout with a pair of QR codes displaying the public and private keys. The security can be further heightened by encrypting the keys with a special password, which is necessary for cases when a paper wallet is stolen or even simply photographed by an attacker.

Such paper wallets are often used to transfer cryptocurrencies as a gift to third parties who do not yet have the appropriate software and accounts set up in blockchain systems. Once in possession of the "paper certificate" with the associated pair of keys and codes, new owners can at any time transfer the crypto funds on said accounts to any of the selected hot wallets and then, if necessary, set up transactions.

The aim in this chapter has not been to provide an exhaustive list of methods for storing cryptocurrency. There are a few less common methods, such as multi-signature wallets or fragmented keys. In the first case, to send a transaction, you must have several private keys – i.e. transferring funds from the wallet requires joint confirmation. In the second method, the private key is broken down into several pieces which are stored in different places. Perhaps in the near future, we will witness completely new methods of storing "digital gold." However, nearly all owners of cryptocurrencies face the same question: what is the best strategy for storing it?

The combined experience of crypto community representatives indicates that the most acceptable and convenient form of storing cryptoassets can be achieved by combining the use of hot and cold wallets. In other words, the primary crypto reserves should be stored in offline hardware wallets and sometimes even on paper, whereas hot wallets are advisable only for holding small amounts in order to be able to conduct transactions as necessary. Conversely, if the owner of the cryptocurrency may be an active stock trader who needs to constantly conduct trading operations, then most of their assets will remain in exchange wallets, despite the additional risk associated with such. "Hodlers" who have made serious long-term investments in cryptocurrencies will certainly keep the majority of their holdings in cold wallets, as they offer greater security.

If we constructed a graph to visualize the interest of the global community in cryptocurrencies, we would see a curve that has its ups and downs at different times. The direction of this graph is influenced by many different factors – social, business, regulatory, and purely technological. To a large extent, the technological aspect will determine whether we will witness in the foreseeable future cryptocurrencies at least somewhat displacing fiat currencies in the world economy. As regards the active development of blockchain, many complex problems still do not have an optimal solution at the moment and are hindering cryptocurrencies from competing on equal footing with their fiat "cohorts." What are the current challenges facing blockchain technology and where should we look for ways to solve them?

Current issues of the blockchain

Most people in developed countries have grown accustomed to using convenient bank cards instead of cash to pay for goods and services. Despite some of the inconveniences that they entail, payment cards have long been firmly established in everyday life. After all, cards can easily be lost or stolen along with the wallet. Unscrupulous sellers can make copies of the cards at the time of transfer, the signature can be forged, and the pin code can be viewed. Home to many gangs of cybercriminals, the internet provides an even more conducive environment for fraud. In 2014 alone, more than USD 16 billion was stolen from bank cards worldwide, and these figures are growing by the year. Why is the global financial industry not showing any sign of hurrying to transition from card payments to the form of cryptocurrency transactions with its seemingly superlative level of operational security?

Prior to answering this question, we need to grasp the scale of the volume of transactions conducted within at least one of the most popular card systems – Visa or Mastercard. On normal days, the financial flows in these systems are measured in thousands of transactions per second. During periods of high activity – e.g. in the days of sales leading up to New Year's – peak loads can reach 20,000–40,000 transactions per second. Now, for comparison's sake, let's calculate what the most popular blockchain payment system – the Bitcoin network – could offer in this regard.

As we remember, blocks in this system have an average size of 1 megabyte, and the average transaction takes about 250–300 bytes, while each new block in the network is formed in an average of ten minutes. Simple calculations show that the throughput of the Bitcoin network works out to about seven transactions per second, after which it should be compared with the speed of processing operations in large card networks. Moreover, this is the only parameter in terms of which we are attempting to compare the two fundamentally different financial technologies. Moreover, this indicator is just a single cog in a larger problem standing in the way of cryptocurrencies acquiring a competitive status on par with fiat means of payment – the problem is called scalability.

Blockchain technology itself has a lot of advantages, which we have considered in great detail over the course of this book. Now, however, we should spend some time discussing some of its shortcomings, and more precisely – about the hurdles preventing the rapid distribution of products based on distributed ledger technology. In general, blockchain products do not have a fantastic degree of scalability, primarily due to the speed with which transactions are confirmed and the constantly increasing volume of the database of blocks, as information previously placed in them cannot be deleted. In other words, if the nature of a task calls for a huge number of microtransactions to be processed rapidly, the blockchain will not cope with this in the best way.

Let's imagine a situation when a payment system built on the basis of blockchain technology registers, for example, the purchase of a cup of coffee in a large chain coffee shop such as Starbucks – i.e. a transaction with a transfer of value amounting to several dollars. First, confirming the transaction means placing it in a block that will be accepted by the entire decentralized network. Then, to be sure, in addition to this block, at least several subsequent blocks should fit into the chain branching off behind it. Undoubtedly, this process will take some time. The question arises: will the buyer and seller wait minutes or even tens of minutes for the payment transaction to receive all the requisite confirmations? In all likelihood, the two counterparties will choose a faster method of payment confirmation.

Let's not overlook another important detail: the number of coffee cups could legitimately be enormous. According to some conjectures, at least 1.5 billion cups of coffee are consumed daily in the world, with a large part being purchased in restaurants and cafes. If payment transactions associated with coffee begin to be placed in the blockchain, the database of blocks will experience growth at inconceivably fast rates. That said, we are talking about a decentralized form of data storage, which means constant replication and synchronization of data between all full network nodes.

The sheer number of such small transactions would surpass the physical capacity of modern blockchain environments, despite the fact that we have only considered transactions for a single product – a cup of coffee. Thus, this begs the conclusion that the classical model of recording and storing transactional information in the blockchain is in no way suitable for registering massive amounts of microtransactions – whether in terms of processing speed or in terms of the volumes of data storage required. What approach could be taken to solving this problem?

One solution may be so-called "sharding." Instead of redundantly copying a complete database of blocks between network participants, the concept of sharding in blockchain technology calls for breaking the database down into a certain number of parts, each of which is copied only to a certain group of network nodes. Maintaining the integrity of a distributed data infrastructure requires accurate mathematical calculations of the number of parts of the complete database, the size of each part, and the number of nodes in each group storing segments of the database. The concept of "integrity" in this case implies close to 100% guarantee that for the purposes of synchronization, each of the nodes of the network will have access at any time to any part of the full database of blocks.

Currently, many developers of blockchain projects are actively exploring the possibilities of implementing the concept of sharding. One of the first developments in this area was announced by the team of developers in the Ethereum project headed by Vitalik Buterin. As yet, however, no workable model of sharding has been presented to the public. Nonetheless, sharding is emphatically not a panacea for "bloating" databases blocks, but only offers some brief respite from the negative impact of this problem. That said, sharding will clearly improve scenarios in blockchain environments where microtransactions are either completely absent or are not the predominant type of transaction. As for blockchain payment systems vying for mass use in everyday life, the concept of the Lightning Network protocol seems a much more promising solution to the problem of scaling.

In the effort to adapt the Bitcoin network to micropayments, another issue arises: the fee. As we have seen, the miners who form blocks in this network are rewarded with transaction fees. In addition to the monetary incentive offered to miners, fees also carry out the important role of protecting against transactional spam, which could theoretically cause the network speed to slacken considerably. Expressed as their fiat equivalent, the fees may add up to sizeable amounts, which makes it altogether pointless to conduct microtransactions. If a cup of coffee, for example, costs two dollars, and the transaction fee for its payment will be close to the amount, how many people would be willing to pay double the price for the pleasure of making the purchase with cryptocurrency? Indeed, the Lightning Network model was developed just for such situations.

In fact, Lightning Network is a second-layer technology built over the blockchain system. Also, this does not only apply to the Bitcoin network, as similar concepts are being developed for other popular blockchain environments.

The network of "lightning transfers" consists of nodes that by pairing off among themselves form bi-directional "payment channels." Each of the two nodes blocks a certain amount of funds for the created channel, the sum of which is its payment throughput. In this case, nodes can form channels with several nodes at the same time, creating a whole network where paths can be formed for fast transit operations with a low fee.

The transfer of funds is carried out by changing the mutual balances on the channel nodes until one of the nodes runs out of funds – i.e. the channel is considered "depleted." At any time, the nodes can close the channel and credit to themselves funds equal to the current settlement balance. This offers a quick and superlatively economical solution to the problem of microtransactions for payments with popular cryptocurrencies. Like with everything else, this model also has its drawbacks, chief among which is the lack of long-term motivation provided for network nodes to maintain payment channels; the remuneration for the nodes is truly quite modest. According to current estimates, the content of the lightning network node brings its owner an income of only about 1% per annum. At the same time, each node of the payment channels must block its own funds in order for the network to operate, thereby remaining constantly online and thus being exposed to the risk of a hacker attack.

Another problem with the way that such networks operate is their potentially excessive centralization, when the most active nodes can accumulate significant cryptocurrency liquidity. Similarly, if a node is disconnected from the network, the funds of other users who have sent their payments via this infrastructure may be blocked for a long time. This network is also not immune to the endeavors of fraudsters, especially if one of the channel nodes disappears from the network for a long time. Nevertheless, the concept of the Lightning Network model continues to show signs of active growth – as of spring 2019, in the Bitcoin network alone there are more than 40,000 payment channels and the growth is ongoing.

It should be added that a Lightning Network model is not the only means of scaling the blockchain. We will not dwell on the technological description of other concepts, such as, for example, directed acyclic graphs or methods of decreasing the transaction size by removing digital electronic signatures from it. It is worth noting only that thus far none of the existing methods has been able to fully solve the problem of throughput or excessive amounts of data storage.

In addition to purely technological problems, blockchain also faces problems of a social nature. As noted in the chapter on bitcoin mining and the description of the proof-of-work protocol, this method of issuing cryptocurrencies is characterized by exceptional energy intensity and indirectly causes additional damage to the environment. Because of its conceptual complexity, many users fail to grasp the advantages and disadvantages of distributed ledger technology. The influence of the cryptocurrency hype has often led to scenarios where isolated representatives of the business community are trying to repurpose their existing projects to accommodate blockchain technology. It should always be borne in mind that such an insufficiently crafted strategy, instead of creating additional value, can destroy even a previously successful business.

Moreover, the regulatory environment is rarely friendly to either the blockchain projects themselves or the methods of their financing – in particular, via ICOs. All indicators seem to suggest that the rigor with which the blockchain industry is regulated will only increase in the future. In addition, let's not forget that the owners of cryptocurrencies are by definition anonymous, so sellers who accept crypto funds for payment will have to comply with regulatory requirements to identify their customers. As for large financial institutions, primarily banks, they in some cases rightly view blockchain technology as a threat to their very existence, since it presumes the decentralization and elimination of financial intermediation. Although in fairness it should be noted that many banks have begun to use blockchain technology to optimize their own costs and improve the competitiveness of their financial products.

At present, we can only state with certainty a few main conclusions: that blockchain is an entirely promising technology, that it has its own fair share of serious problems, and that the best minds from the global mathematical sciences community and the IT industry are laboring to remedy them. Admittedly, these issues cannot be resolved overnight, so one should not expect rapid breakthroughs – the crypto community will solve problems step by step. And then, when a certain critical mass of useful ideas, tools, models and concepts is achieved, their combined effect will be able to get a few steps closer to actually solving the problems which blockchain technology is currently facing.

New world view (conclusion)

It has been more than ten years since the genesis block appeared in the first blockchain network of the Bitcoin project. This event marked the emergence of a whole high-tech industry and has since impacted the lives of many people. Some managed to make a pretty penny on early investments in cryptocurrency, and others managed to promote ideas that interested investors at the right time after raising significant amounts via an ICO. And there were those who took the developers at their word and invested in new cryptocoins, which then depreciated within the span of a few months. The blockchain industry can be a source of elation and disappointment, build up hope and reduce it to naught, incite radical changes in the philosophy of building business models, as well as lead researchers into technological deadlocks, which, at first glance, seem to be a complete dead end. In short, there is a normal evolutionary process that inevitably accompanies any truly viable innovative phenomenon.

Some people believe that blockchain technology has more questions than answers, but for now, its ten years of existence seem too short a time to draw for drawing such hasty conclusions. American physicist, former US Secretary of Energy, and Nobel laureate Steven Chu once said: "The Stone Age did not end because we ran out of stones." Of course, blockchain technology is currently going through its own "Stone Age" of sorts. However, the principles of openly exchanging information which have been adopted in the blockchain industry give every reason to assume that its development will be very rapid. First of all, this will be facilitated by the combined efforts of everyone involved in the process – entrepreneurs, engineers, and scientists. Whether blockchain will further evolve to its own "bronze" or "iron" age will be left for time to determine. One thing is certain: we are dealing not only with a new concept of accounting, storage, and transfer of value, but also with a new technological philosophy capable of introducing a tectonic shift in the model of social and business relationships which humans have known for millennia.

At its core, it boils down to a question of transforming the concept of mediation. If it does not eliminate this role completely, blockchain can at least significantly reduce its dominance by offering the concept of decentralized relationships between counterparties. What consequences could this have? Eliminating the intermediary's margin can release unspeakable potential for redistributing precious human and financial resources from unproductive purposes to more creative ones. Admittedly, not all forms of mediation necessarily provide ballast for the global economy, but there are a number of typical mediation operations, which humanity can safely strike out of the equation. Moreover, one of the primary catalysts of such can be the blockchain technology, which makes it possible for projects to implement fundamentally new concepts in terms of their architectural ideology, thus enabling far-reaching disintermediation in the field of commercial and other services.

As for the role of the state and financial regulation, due account should be given to the fact that the natural conservatism of bureaucratic institutions will tend to hinder the development of blockchain technology rather than promote it. We can only hope that some governments will adopt a strategy of assuming reasonable risks in relation to the regulation of the crypto environment. In turn, this will contribute to further progress in the development of both the financial sector and service infrastructure as a whole. This will give an undeniable advantage over countries that adhere to the protective principles of classical financial models, which guarantee them the semblances of stability as well as inevitable stagnation in technological development. In any case, it would be unwise to ignore the strategic trends in the global information technology industry, as this will inevitably lead to technologically falling behind the rest of the world – not to mention that the infrastructure will deteriorate.

For now, let's give the statistics the chance to speak for themselves. In 2018 alone, the number of blockchain developers in the world has increased 33 times, whereas the demand from commercial companies for specialists in blockchain solutions increased by 517% over the same period. LinkedIn – a social network for the business community – published its research data, which named blockchain developers named the most in-demand specialists in the American labor market. Many universities around the world are opening departments for training specialists for the blockchain industry, but this process is still developing, albeit not at the rate that the global IT business would like to see. All of this attests to a large-scale interest in blockchain technology in its own right as well as to the fact that many people increasingly view blockchain as a key to further development in the business and social environment.

Returning to the quote of the American lawyer Nicholas Klein from the beginning of the book, let's try to determine whether a monument to the blockchain will ever be erected. In the first ten years of the technology's existence, it was subjected to a full range of emotions from the community:

from indifference or restrained optimism to aggression and truly biblical fanaticism. It was anathematized by governments and state regulators, but exulted by proponents of libertarian or anarchist ideas. Various analysts tagged crypto projects as financial bubbles and pyramids, but there were also those who heralded a new image of a world that would never be the same. Some authoritative visionaries predicted that the value of bitcoin would reach millions in the coming years, whereas others projected an inglorious demise. And someone even calculated that the Bitcoin project had been "buried" on no fewer than 334 occasions, and that number could still increase.

One thing is for sure: blockchain technology is at the dawn of its era. Is it destined to alter the centralized methods commonplace in the management of business, governments, and society as a whole? Will cryptocurrencies get a chance to at least partially displace the classical means of payment currently in circulation? Will this help to make the processes of transferring value more transparent and equitable for society? If most of these issues end up being resolved, then we can hope that grateful descendants will indeed erect a monument to the blockchain.

Tallinn, Estonia
2018–2019

CPSIA information can be obtained
at www.ICGtesting.com
Printed in the USA
BVHW091946040521
606416BV00010B/1508